Itty Bitty Quilts

CONNECTING THREADS

Itty Bitty Quilts ©2015

#46239

ISBN: 978-1-62767-093-7

Connecting Threads Director: Teri Stillwell

Pattern Designer: Mari Martin

Photography: Amy Cave, John Cranford

Photography Stylist: Dawn van Buuren

Book Designer: Jenna Buescher-Hill

Editors: Teri Stillwell, Alisha Runckel, Jamila Clarke

Technical Pattern Editors: Ann Johnson, Mari Martin

Printed in the United States of America

Contents

I LOVE celebrating, especially seasons and holidays. Wouldn't it be a delightful thing to have just a little something in the home to remind us of a special day, or season to look forward to? The snow of January, love in February, or perhaps the enchantment of Halloween with all of its hilariously scary imagery.

What if we bundled all of that into teeny, weeny quilts? Quilts that can be constructed in an hour or two, start to finish—and can be displayed and enjoyed through every season and holiday of the year? My *Itty Bitty Quilts* book is for everyone who loves to celebrate the holidays and seasons as much as I do. Have fun with these adorable projects; I hope you enjoy making them as much as I enjoyed designing them!

Delightfully yours,

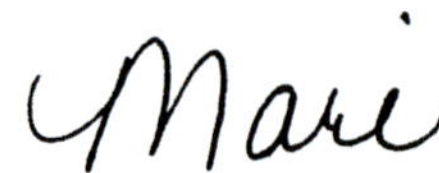

How to Use This Book

The projects in this book use appliqué. There are many different ways to approach this technique, including freezer paper and fusible—both of which are demonstrated in the following pages. We will also cover a finishing method of appliqué: the hidden appliqué stitch.

Practice your appliqué skills by sewing up one, or all of the Itty Bitty Quilts in this book. Just like our other exclusive Connecting Threads patterns, we offer cutting suggestions as well as full-sized appliqué templates located in the back of this book.

Fabric Supply List

Use your stash, or purchase this Quilter's Candy Stack.

To make all of the Itty Bitty Quilts in this book, we have chosen a number of fabrics from our Quilter's Candy Basics collection to make fabric selection easy for you. To purchase this stack of fabrics, you can order online at **ConnectingThreads.com** or by calling our customer service at 1-800-574-6454.

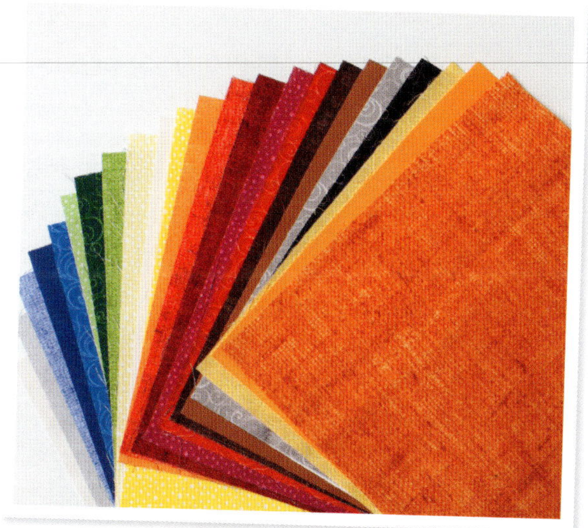

Itty Bitty Quilt Stack
Contains 35, 10" squares of Quilter's Candy Fabrics. *Limited to stock on hand, while supplies last.*
8666 Stack **Your Cost $14.28**

You will also need

- ¾ yard of 3908 Solid – Black
- ½ yard of 7690 Osnaburg – Natural
- ½ yard of 6685 Lotta Dots - White on White
- ½ yard of 5714 Swirls - White on White

Required Materials

Required Materials: A) Lite Steam-A-Seam 2®, B) Clover Curved Awl, C) Roxanne Glue-Baste-It, D) a variety of hand-sewing and embroidery needles, E) paper cutting scissors F) Fons & Porter Mechanical Fabric Pencil, G) appliqué scissors, H) #12 Pearl Cotton or Embroidery Thread, I) Thread.

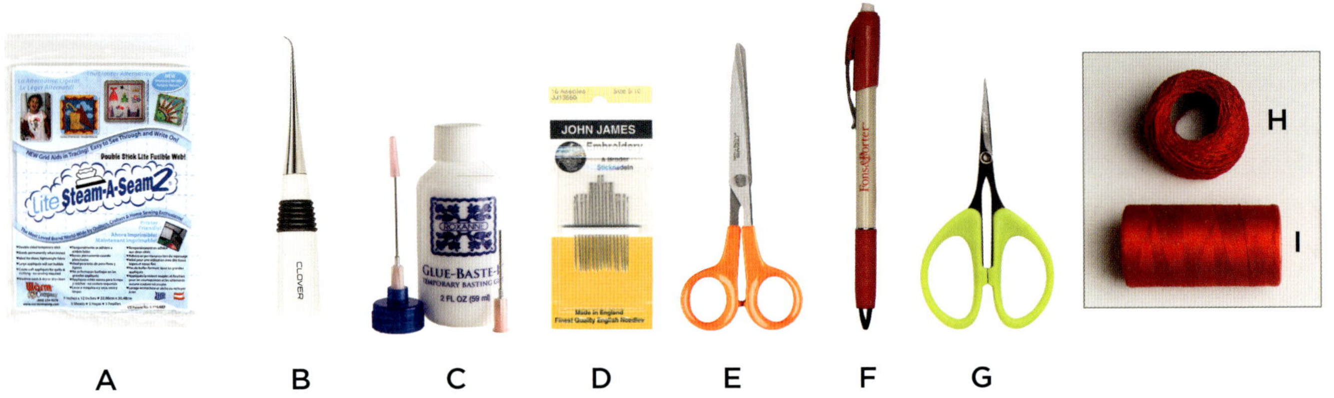

Other Useful Tools

Optional Tools: A) Clover Wonder Clips, B) Spray Sizing, C) Detail paintbrush, D) Kim Diehl's Best Appliqué Freezer Paper, E) Clover Mini Iron.

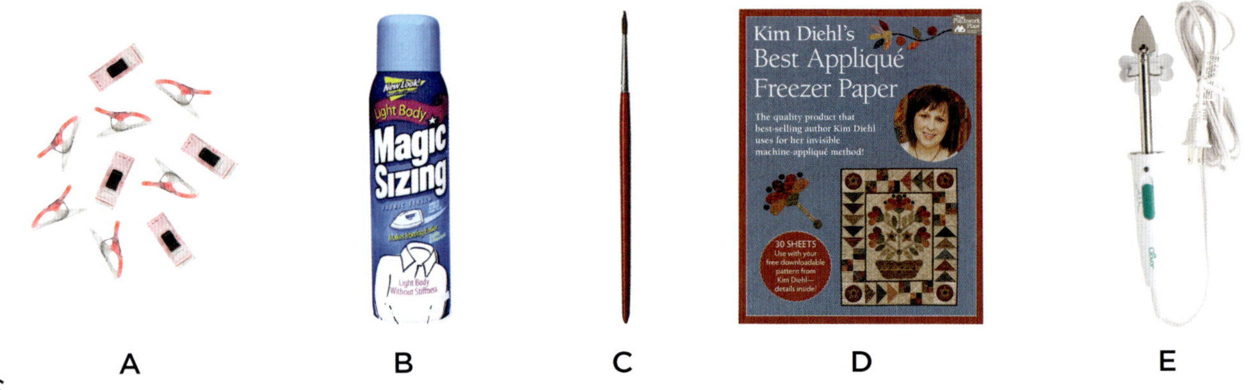

General Instructions

We encourage breaking the rules, but there are a few things you might want to keep in mind. Please read through all of the instructions carefully before beginning a project. Every effort has been made to ensure the accuracy of the patterns. All instructions use a ¼″ seam allowance unless otherwise stated. All fabrics are sewn right sides together (RST), unless otherwise stated.

Need help with any of the techniques used?

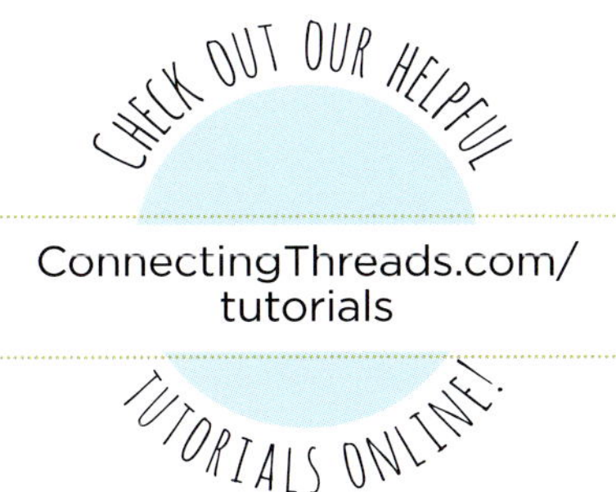

Precut Terminology

- Charms = 5″ squares
- Fat Quarters = 18″ x 22″
- Fat Eighths = 9″ x 18″
- Stacks = 10″ squares
- Strips = 2½″ wide x width of fabric

Cutting Fabric

Helpful suggestions with cutting diagrams are provided for each project in the back of the book.

Common Quilting Acronyms

- FQ = fat quarter
- FE = fat eighth
- HST = half-square triangle
- LOF = length of fabric
- LOFQ = length of fat quarter
- QST = quarter-square triangle
- RS = right side
- RST = right sides together
- WS = wrong side
- WST = wrong sides together
- WOFQ = width of fat quarter
- WOF = width of fabric
- QAYG = quilt as you go

Yardage and Fabric Requirements

Yardage is diagrammed on a 40″ width, selvage to selvage. Fat quarters are diagrammed on a 20″ width, and stacks are diagrammed on a 10″ square.

Squaring Up Blocks

To square up a block using the 45° line on the ruler, place the 45° line on the diagonal corners of the square and trim the horizontal and vertical sides.

Pressing Tips

- Press in the direction of the arrows. If no arrows are provided, press towards the darker fabric.
- Do not slide the iron over the pieces, as this can stretch the fabric. Instead, press and lift the iron off of the fabric.

The Perfect ¼" Seam

A perfect, finished ¼" seam allowance is achieved by sewing slightly less than a ¼". This is called a scant ¼". The purpose for this is to allow space the fold will need when the seam is pressed.

Make sure the measurements on the sewing machine and ¼" foot are accurate before sewing. Remove the presser foot and measure with a ruler. Lower the needle and place the edge of the ruler directly in front of the needle. Note where the ¼" line on the ruler falls and mark. Laying masking tape or painter's tape on the line established can be a visual guideline for sewing. Another option is to use ¼" graph paper.

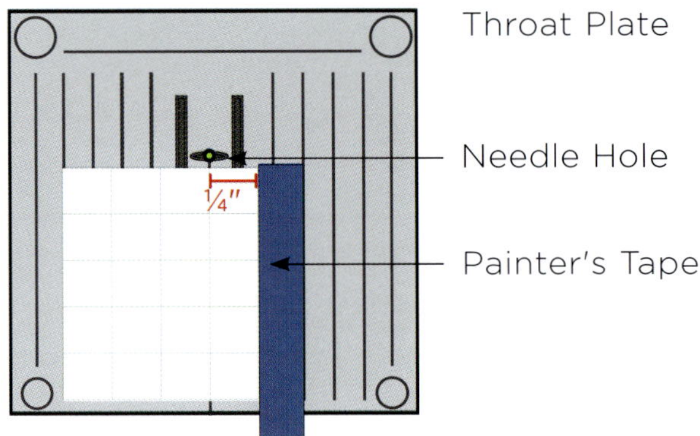

The Test

Once your machine is set up for the perfect ¼" seam, cut three 1½" squares. Sew them together as shown and press the seams away from the center. Measure the center square. If it measures 1" between seams, you have a perfect ¼" seam allowance!

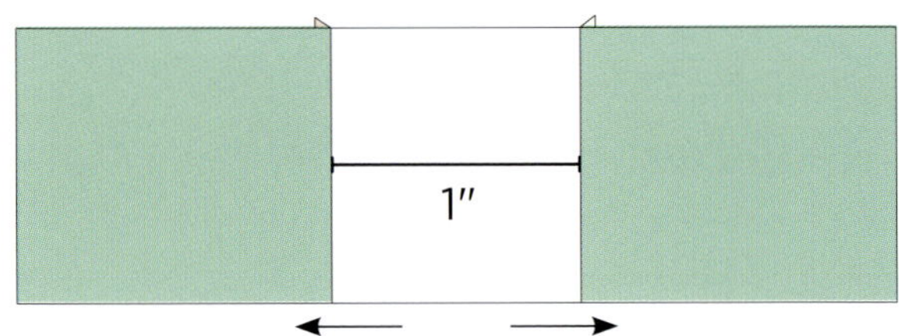

Finishing Your Itty Bitty Quilts

Sew On a Hanging Sleeve

Create a hanging sleeve for the back of your individual Itty Bitty Quilts with these five simple steps:

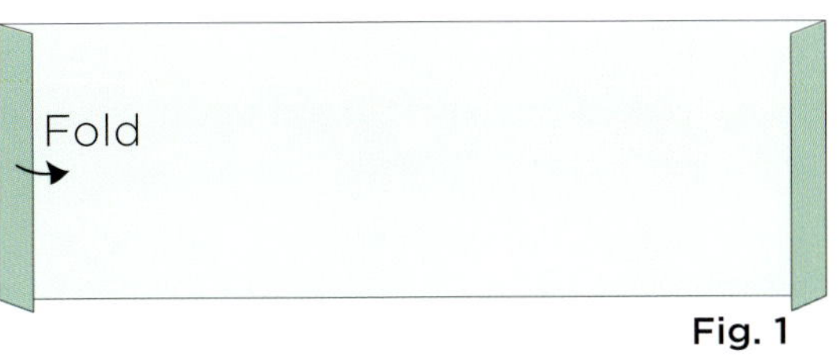

Fig. 1

1. Cut a piece of fabric to 2″ x 6½″. Fold ¼″ on the 2″ edge to the wrong side and press. (Fig. 1)

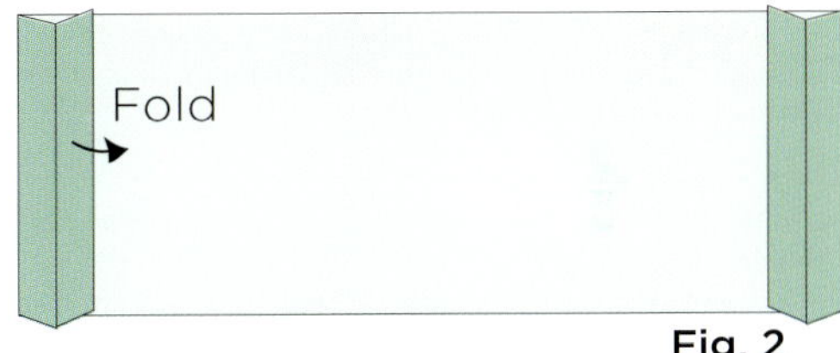

Fig. 2

2. Fold the 2″ edge again to the wrong side ¼″ and press. (Fig. 2)

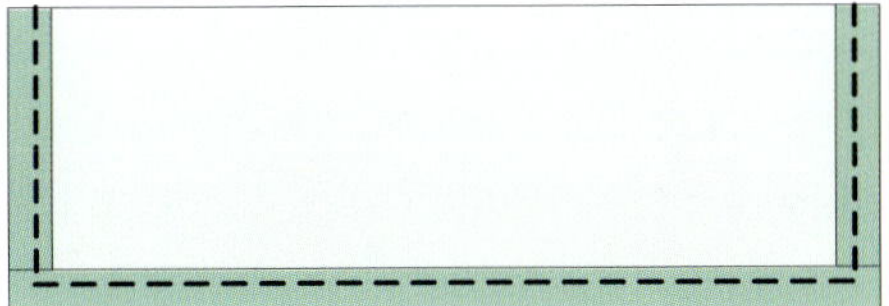
Fig. 3

3. Fold the bottom edge up ¼″ and press. Sew ⅛″ along the three folded edges. (Fig. 3)

4. Lay the sleeve on the back side of the quilt, wrong side down, aligning the top raw edges. Sew the sleeve ⅛″ from the top of your Itty Bitty Quilt.

5. Whipstitch the bottom of the sleeve to your quilt back, being careful not to sew through to the front of your quilt. Bind. (Fig. 4)

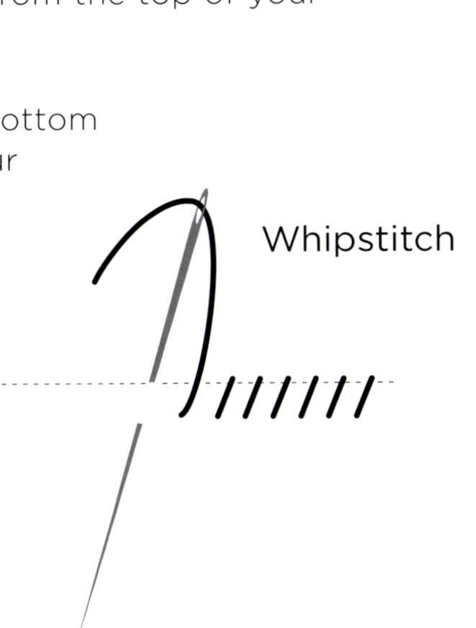

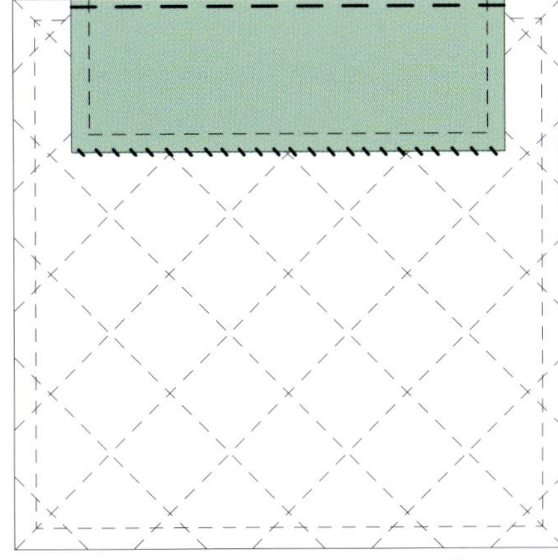
Fig. 4

Binding

The quilts within this book are bound using a 2″ wide binding that is cut on the crosswise grain unless otherwise specified. A traditional French-fold method is recommended without folding the raw edges. There is enough yardage to complete the outer edges of the quilt plus an additional 10″ for mitering each corner. The purpose for adding binding to a quilt is to encase the raw edges of the layers, thus giving the quilt a lovely, finished look.

Binding involves several steps that include making the binding, attaching it to the front of the quilt, and finishing by wrapping it over the raw-edges and stitching it down on the back.

1. Cut the selvages off fabric before constructing the binding. Lay two binding strips right sides together perpendicular to one another, leaving a slight overlap on each end. Stitch diagonally (dashed line) from one inset corner to another. Cut the corner off, leaving a ¼″ seam allowance (solid line).

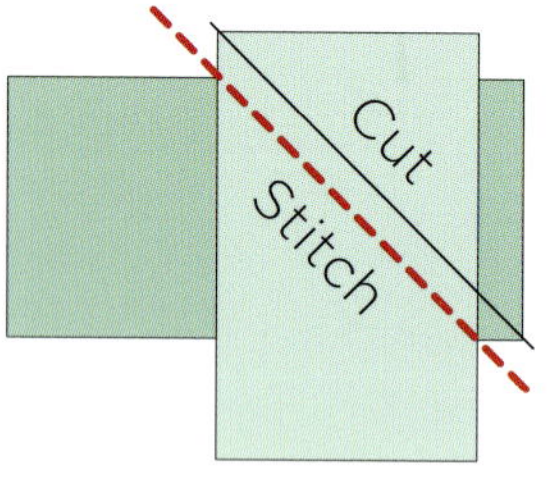

2. Continue sewing binding strips together in this way. Lay the continuous strip out and press all seams open. Trim seam allowance points to the raw edge.

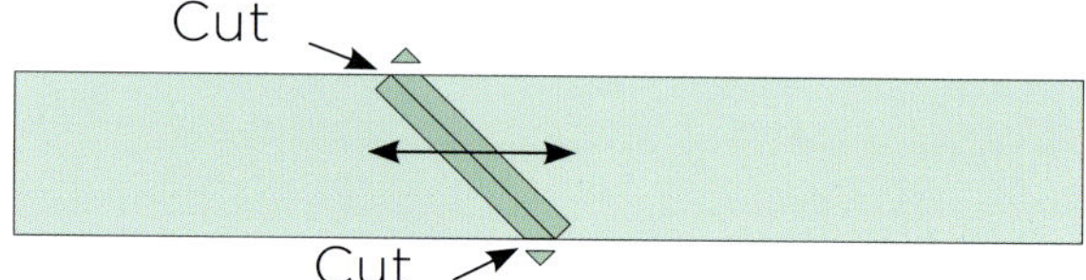

3. From the wrong side of the binding, fold the right end corner over toward the bottom of the strip creating a 45° angle. Press.

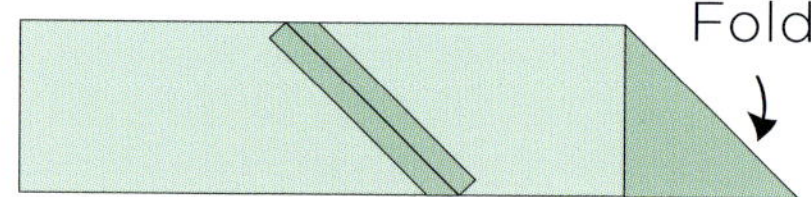

4. Cut the corner off, leaving a ¼″ edge along the fold.

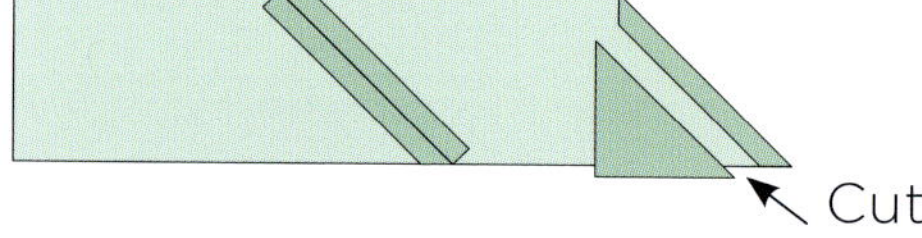

5. Fold the binding in half lengthwise WST and press.

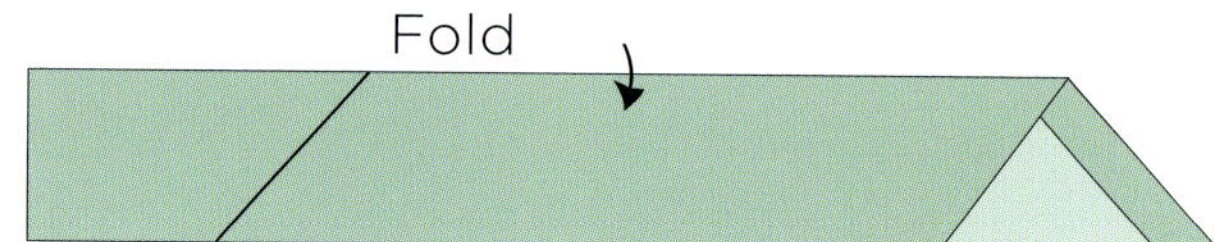

6. Open the strip and lay the 45° angled edge along the edge of the quilt. Stitch down ⅛", 3"– 4".

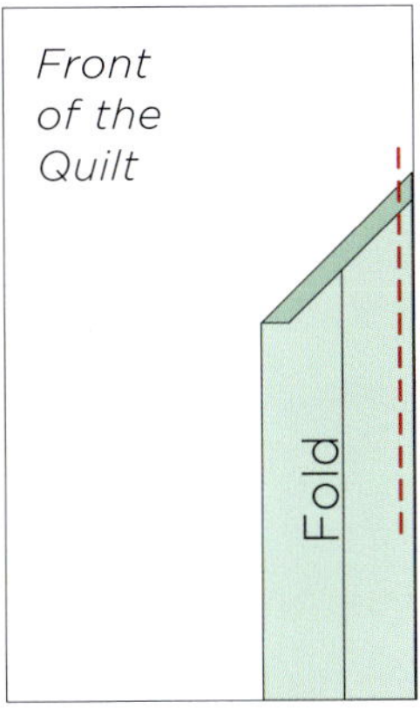

7. Fold the binding back over and begin sewing 2" past the folded edge on the RS of the binding. Continue sewing around the quilt at ¼".

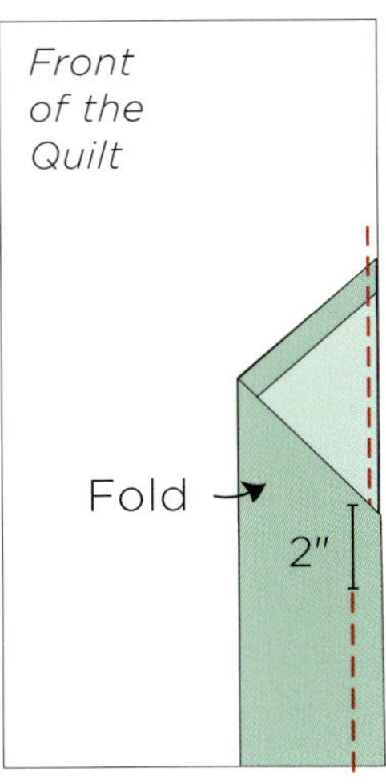

Managing Binding Corners

8. Sew to within ¼" of the edge of the quilt and stop. Lock the stitch by back-stitching, cut threads, and pull fabric from the machine. Fold the binding up to create a 45° angle at the fold.

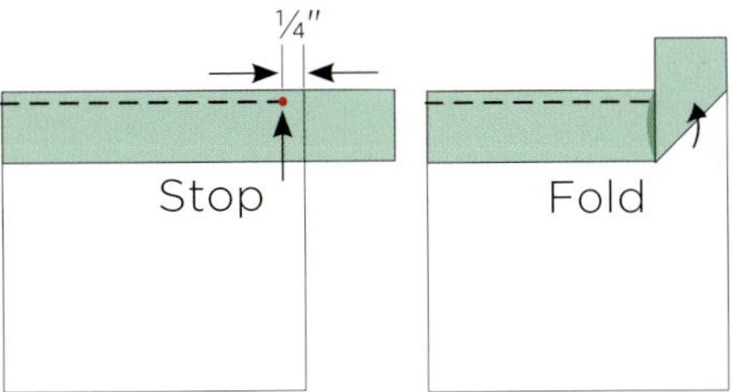

9. Bend the vertical binding down so it creates a fold at the raw edge of the quilt. Starting at the top edge, sew a ¼" seam along the side of the quilt. Repeat for each corner. *Hint:* sew the stitches closer together at the corners to secure them.

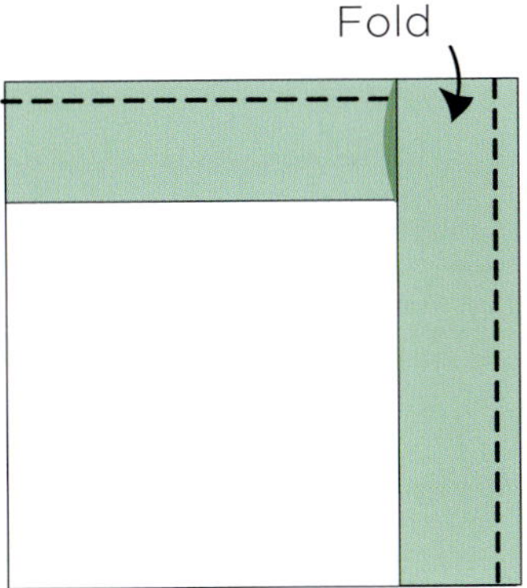

Finishing the Binding

10. When approaching the starting point stop stitching within 4" of the beginning edge. Leave the needle in the down position and cut the end of the binding, leaving enough length to tuck inside the pocket created at the beginning.

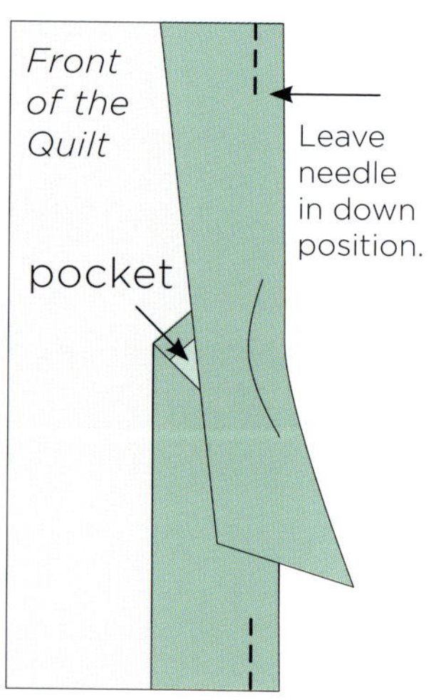

11. Tuck binding into the pocket and continue sewing the seam.

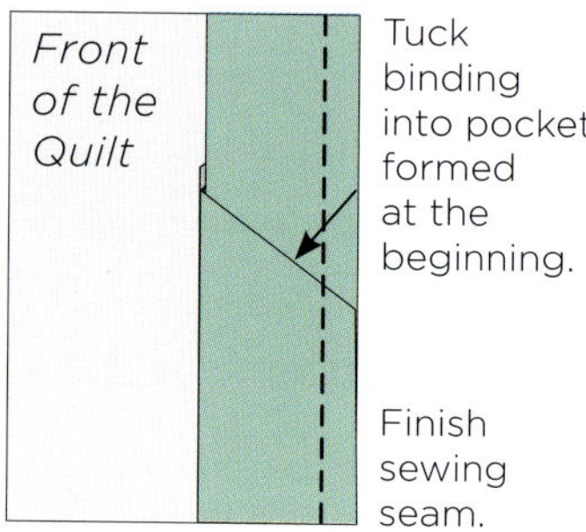

12. Fold binding back over the seam and press the seam only, gently. Wrap the binding around the seam to the back side of the quilt, pin or clip binding and hand sew it down hiding the stitch line. *Hint:* sew the stitches closer together at the corners to secure them.

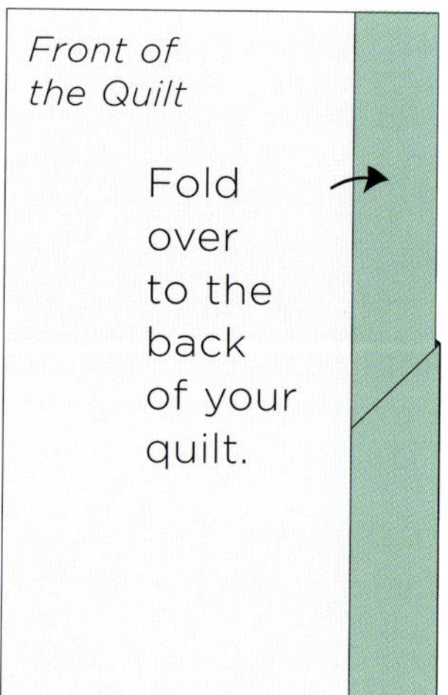

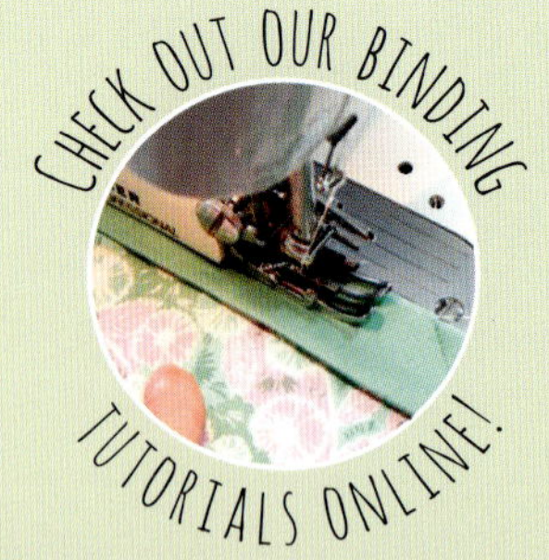

Need more help with binding?

Visit ConnectingThreads.com/tutorials and click on Binding Basics for more detailed photographs and instructions.

Embroidery Stitches

Stem Stitch

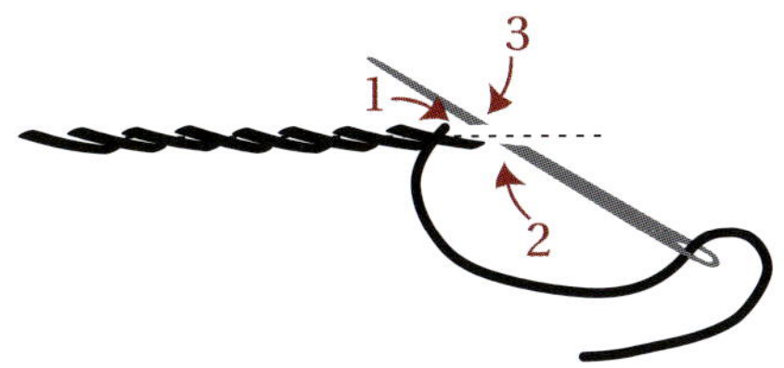

Back Stitch

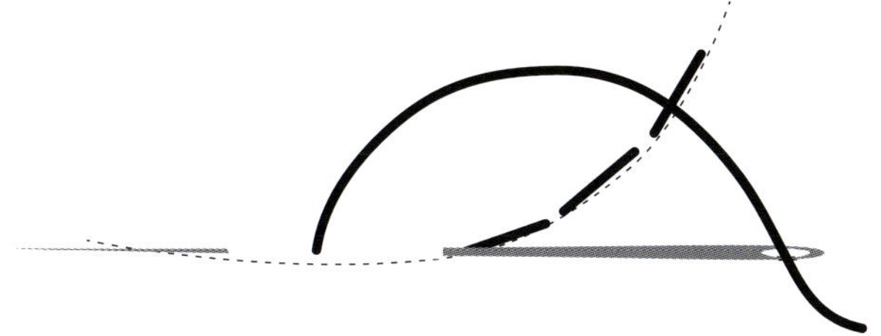

Blanket Stitch

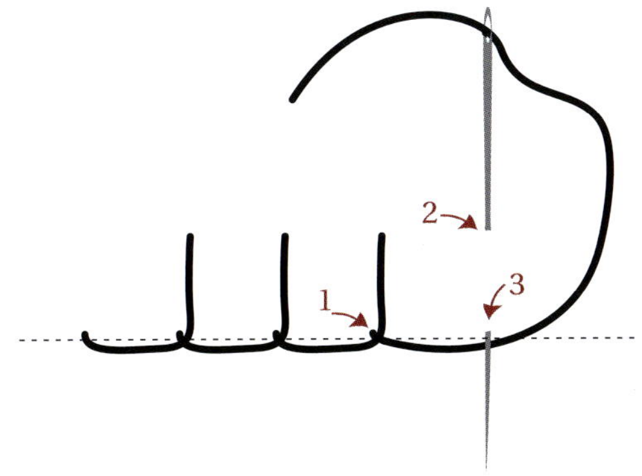

Whipstitch

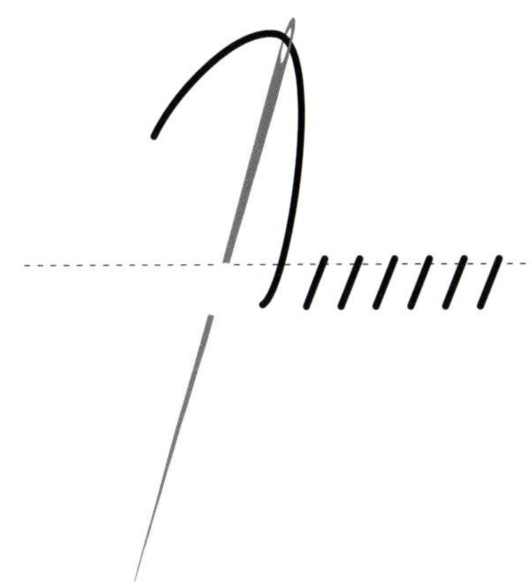

Satin Stitch

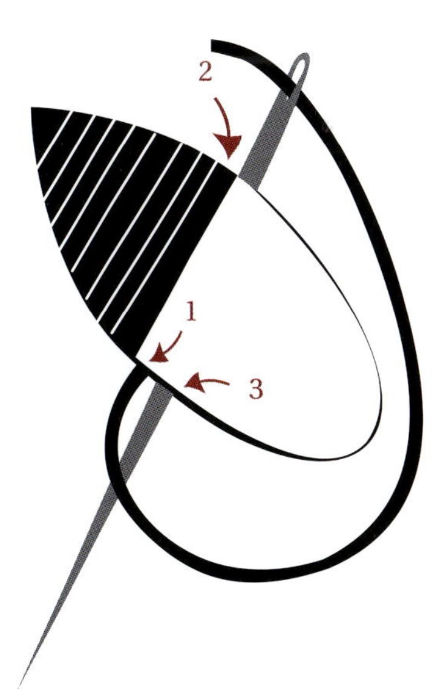

Appliqué Method: Freezer Paper

1. With the waxy side of the freezer paper facing down, trace the appliqué template. Be aware that this method requires reversed templates. (Fig. 1)

2. Cut the template out along the drawn lines. Place the template with the waxy side on the wrong side of the fabric and press well. (Fig. 2)

3. Cut the fabric away from the template leaving a ¼" seam allowance around the perimeter of the freezer paper. (Fig. 3)

4. On inset curves, trim fabric away to ⅛". (Fig. 4)

5. Clip slightly on the inset curves, making sure the cuts are not completely to the paper. (Fig. 5)

6. Apply sizing approx. 1½" along the length of the seam allowance with a paint brush. (Fig.6)

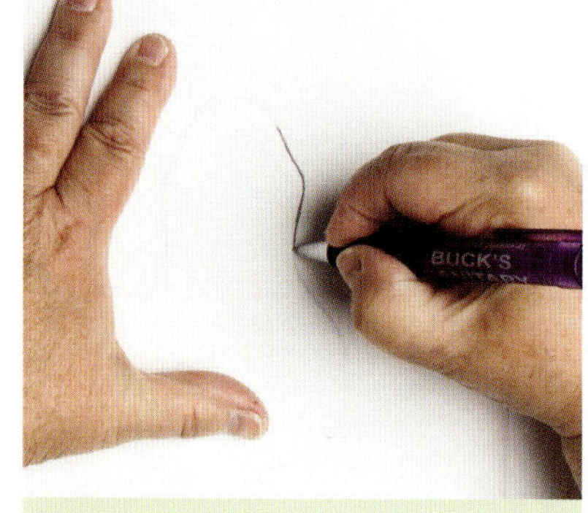

Fig. 1

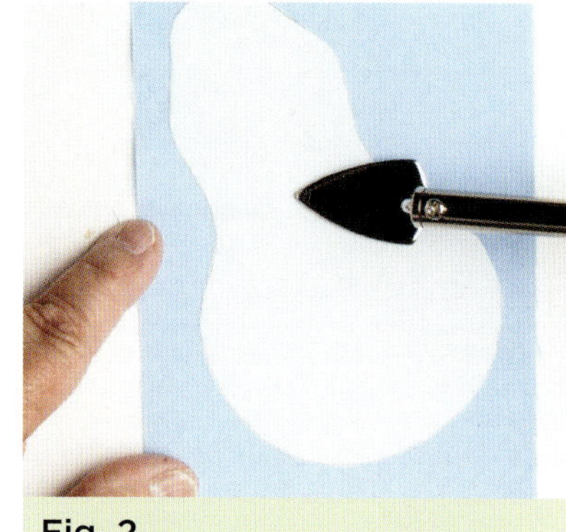
Fig. 2

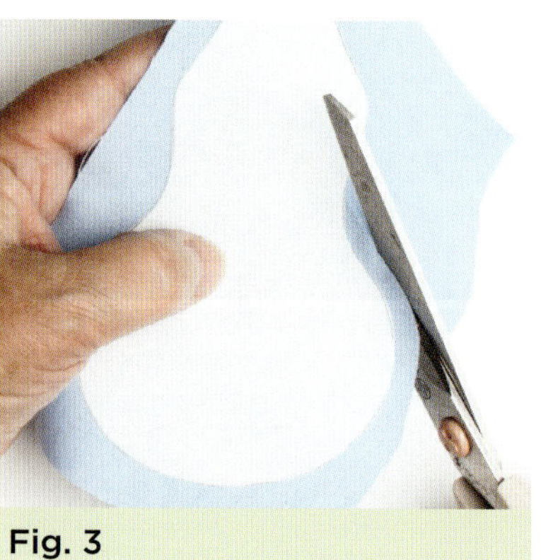
Fig. 3

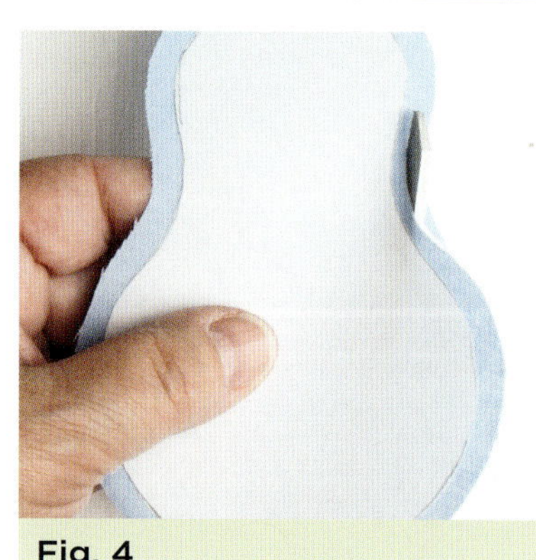
Fig. 4

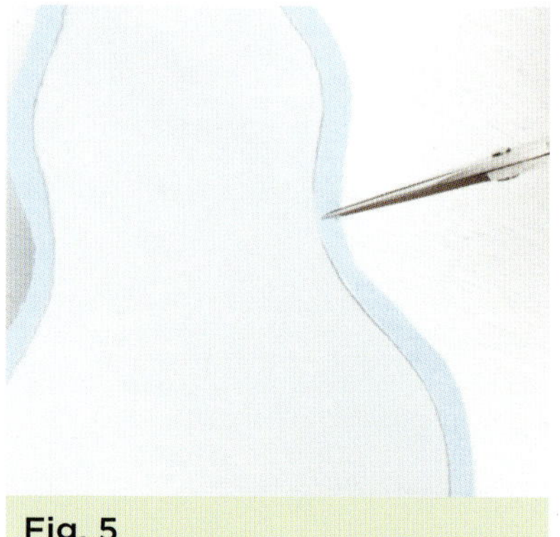
Fig. 5

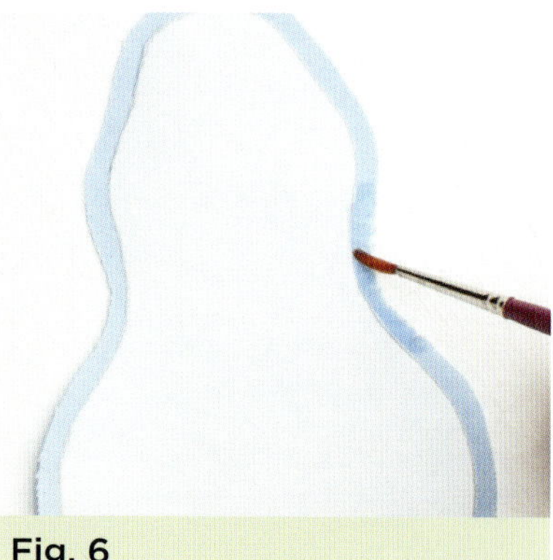
Fig. 6

7. Run the point of the mini iron under the wet fabric, gently pressing it onto the freezer paper. (Fig. 7)

8. Using the same process, press convex curves spacing them out as shown. Then go back and press the area in between to achieve a smooth edge around the paper. (Fig. 8)

9. With an awl, gently ease the point between the paper and fabric to release the paper from the fabric. (Figs. 9a, 9b)

10. Repress any uneven disturbed edges. The appliqué piece is now ready to be sewn. (Fig. 10)

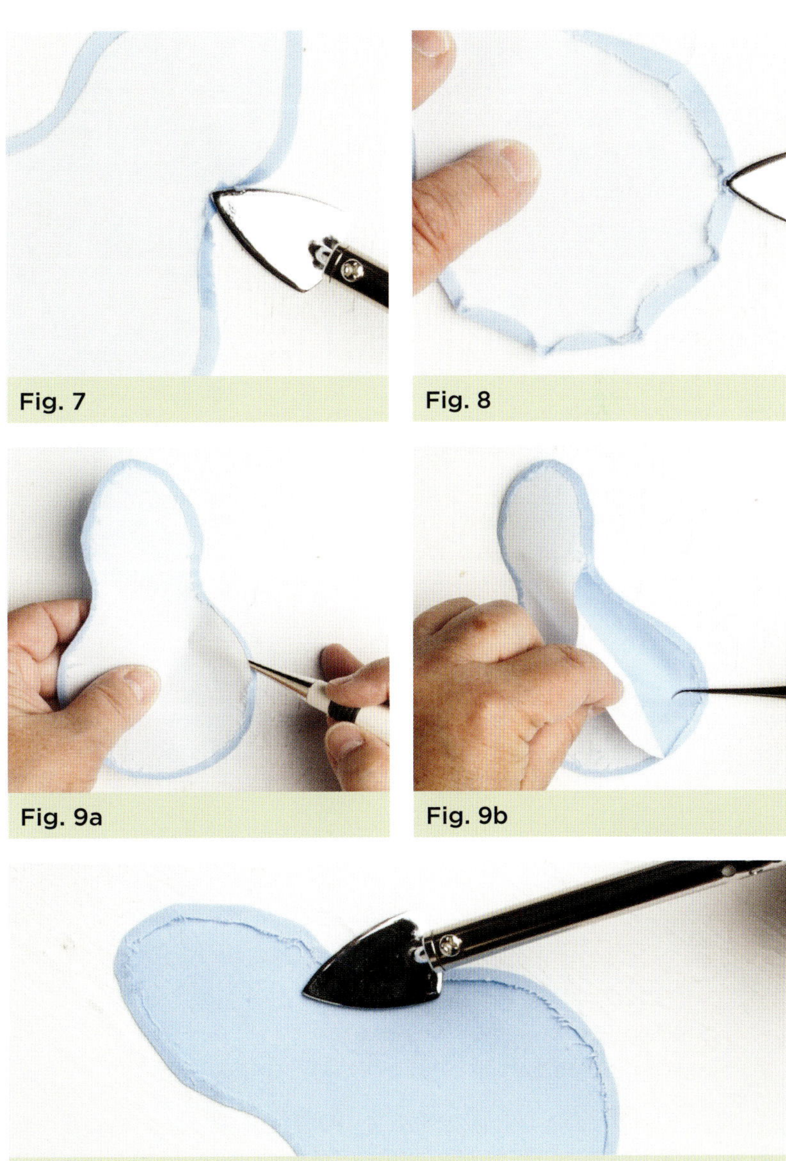

Fig. 7

Fig. 8

Fig. 9a

Fig. 9b

Fig. 10

Appliqué Method: Fusible

1. Draw the image on the paper side of the fusible product. Be aware the template needs to be reversed for this method. (Fig. 1)

2. Place the fusible on the wrong side of the fabric and press following manufacturer's directions. (Fig. 2)

3. When cool, cut away excess paper and fabric from the perimeter following the drawn line. (Fig. 3)

4. Remove the paper from the appliqué piece. It will leave the fusible material behind on the fabric. If pressed too long, the fusible will dissolve. If not long enough, the paper will not release from the fabric easily. (Fig. 4)

5. Lay the appliqué on the right side of the fabric with the fusible side of the appliqué piece facing down and press following the manufacturers directions. (Fig. 5)

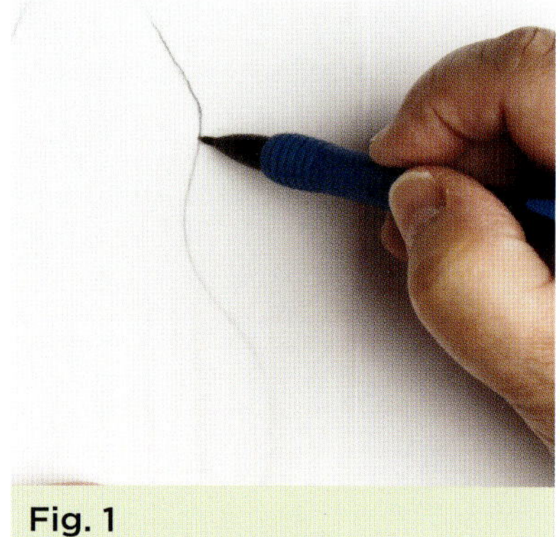

Fig. 1

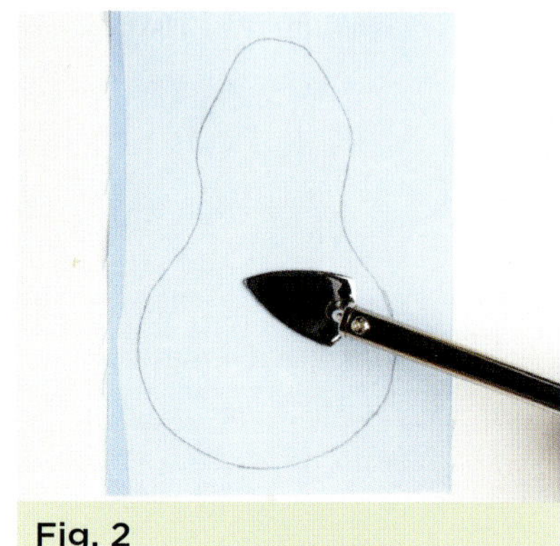

Fig. 2

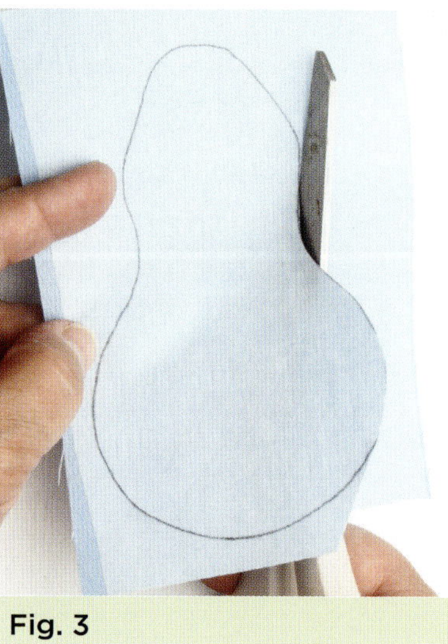

Fig. 3

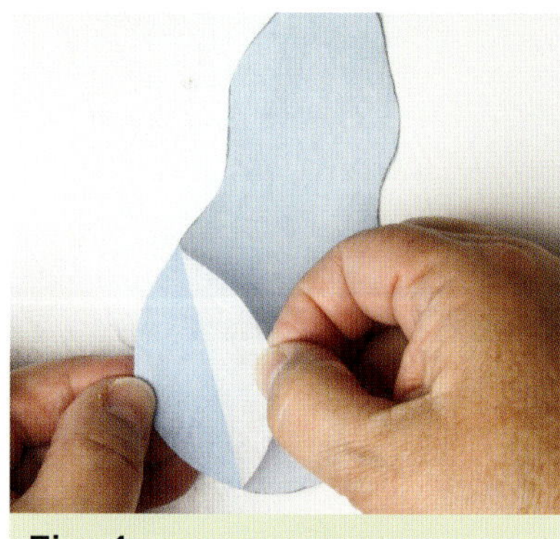

Fig. 4

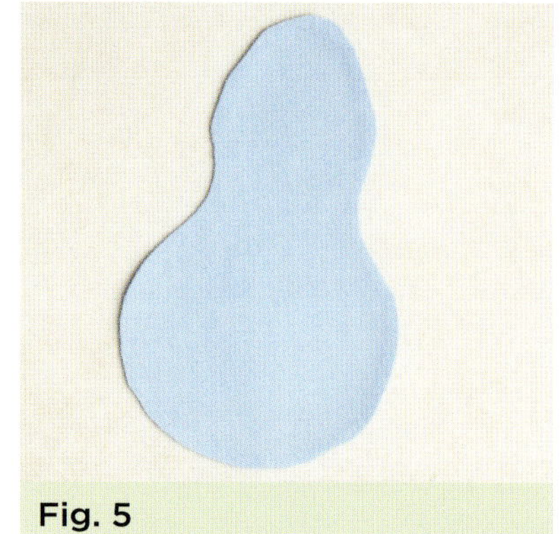

Fig. 5

The Hidden Appliqué Stitch

Once the appliqué shape is prepared, it is sewn to the background fabric using a machine or hand stitch. To achieve a hidden appliqué stitch by hand, follow these simple instructions:

1. Baste the appliqué shape to the background fabric using matching thread, pins, or glue. (A red, contrasting thread is used here for demonstration purposes.) Run a needle from the backside of your appliqué piece, leading it through the fold in the edge. This will hide the knot. (Fig. 1)

2. Run the needle through the background fabric and through the back of the appliqué seam, piercing through the fold again. (Fig. 2)

3. Continue this process around the perimeter of the appliqué piece. This technique results in unseen stitches, thus giving the appliqué a crisp, clean finish. (Fig. 3)

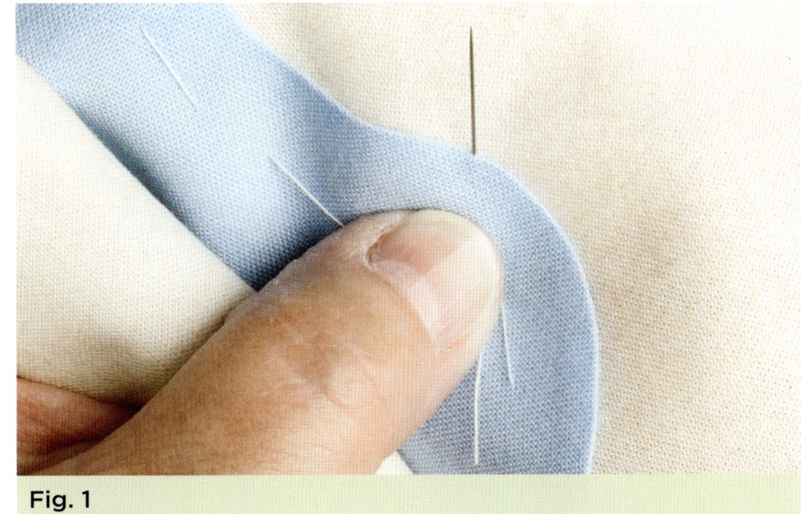

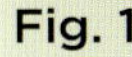
Fig. 1

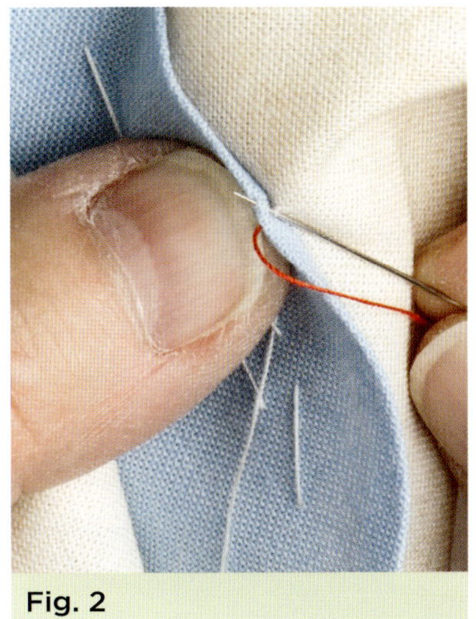
Fig. 2

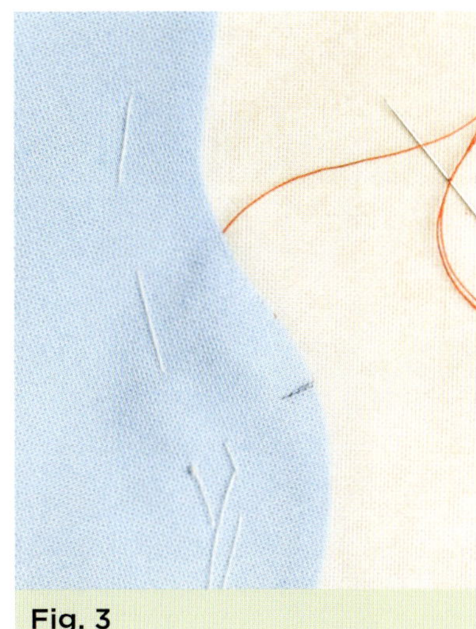
Fig. 3

Itty Bitty January Snowman

Approx. finished size: 6½" square

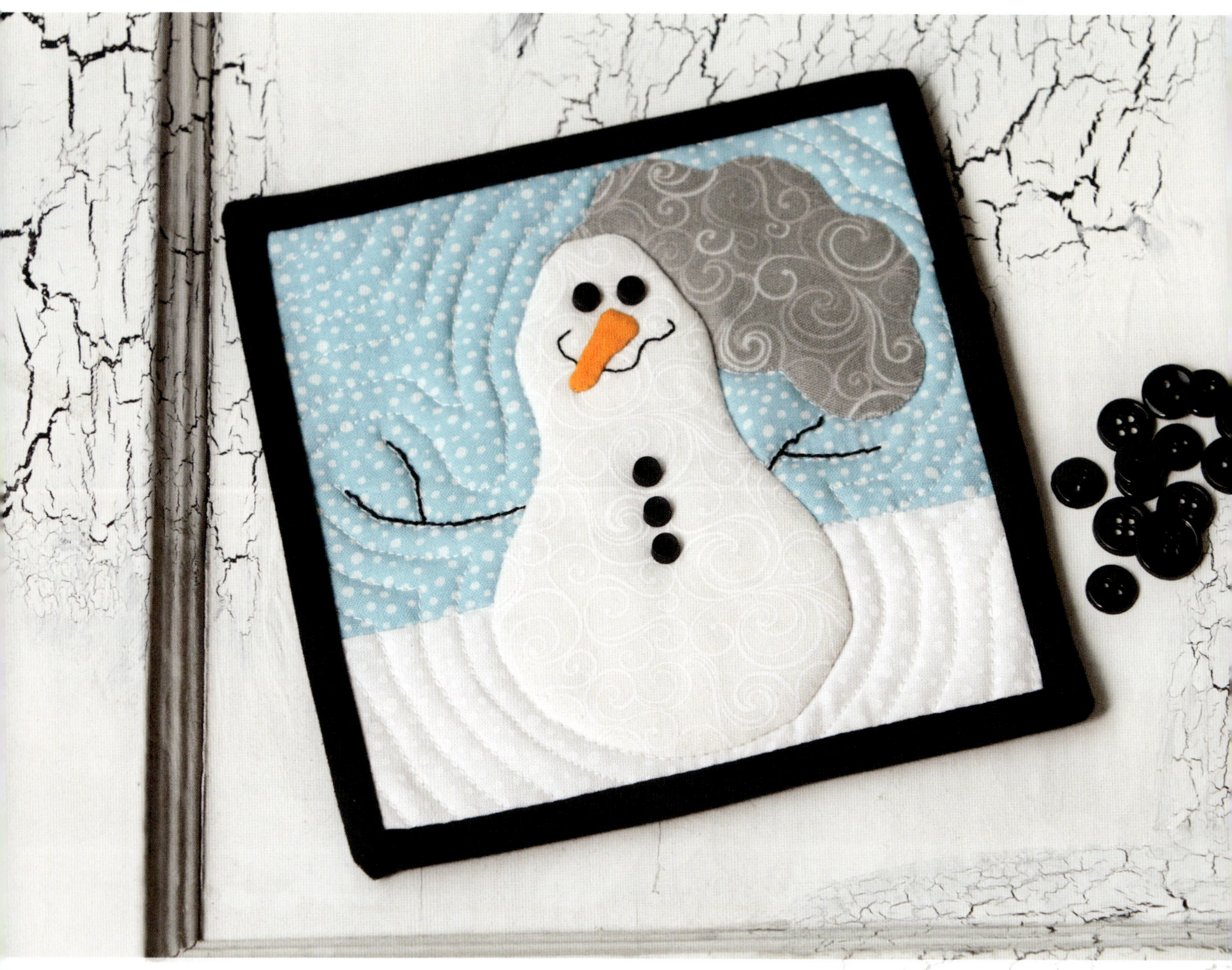

 Shown in Quilter's Candy Basics by Connecting Threads.

Connecting Threads Fabrics Used

- **Fabric 1:** Lotta Dots - Ocean Mist
- **Fabric 2:** Lotta Dots - White on White
- **Fabric 3:** Swirls - Stone
- **Fabric 4:** Swirls - White on White
- **Fabric 5:** Solid - Orangina
- **Fabric 6:** Solid - Black

Binding

Construct the binding for all twelve Itty Bitty Quilts when the January quilt is made. The remainder of Fabric 6 is used for appliqué pieces needed for other Itty Bitty Quilts.

Additional Supplies

- 21294 Lite Steam-A-Seam 2®
- Black embroidery floss
- Grey embroidery floss (optional)
- (5) ¼" Black buttons
- Fusible woven interfacing (optional)

Please Note

Cutting suggestions are listed on pages 68 - 73.

Appliqué templates are listed on pages 74 - 78.

Cutting Instructions

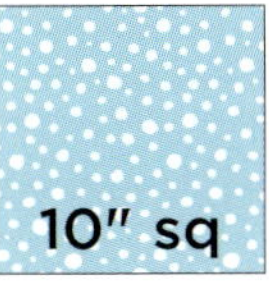

Fabric 1
A - One 4½" x 6½"

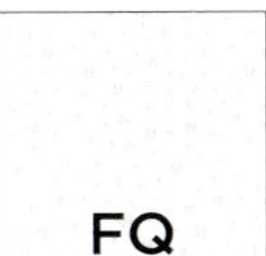
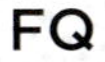

Fabric 2
B - One 2½" x 6½"

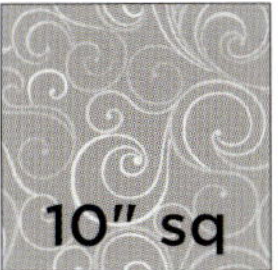

Fabric 3
C - One from template

FQ

Fabric 4
D - One from template

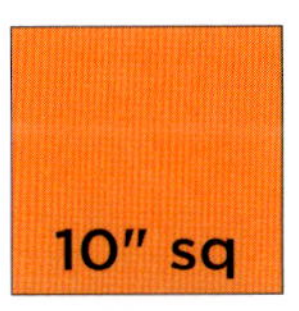

Fabric 5
E - One from template

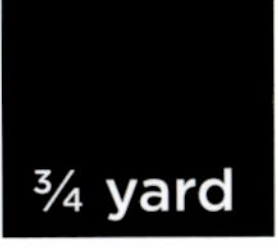

Fabric 6
Binding - at least 372" of a continuous 2" strip. (This is the binding for all Itty Bitty Quilts in this series, as well as all appliqués.) See page 72 for cutting suggestions.

Backing: An additional 9" square

Directions

1. Sew **A** and **B** together. Press. *Hint:* use fusible woven interfacing for the back of **A/B** to hide embroidery stitches.

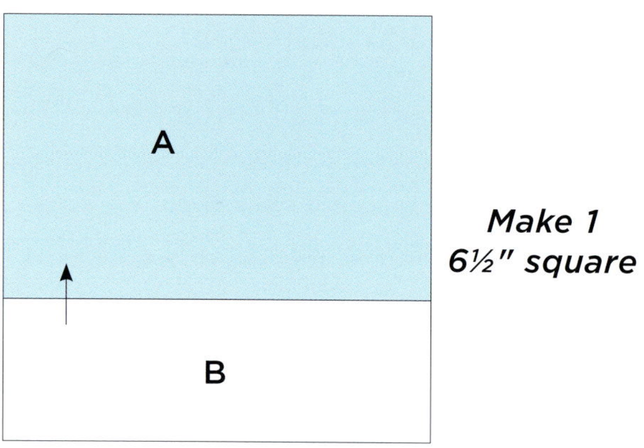

Make 1
6½" square

Appliqué

2. Using appliqué method of choice, appliqué in the following order, **C**, **D** and **E** to the **A/B** unit. *Hint:* place a thin piece of batting under the snowman for added dimension.

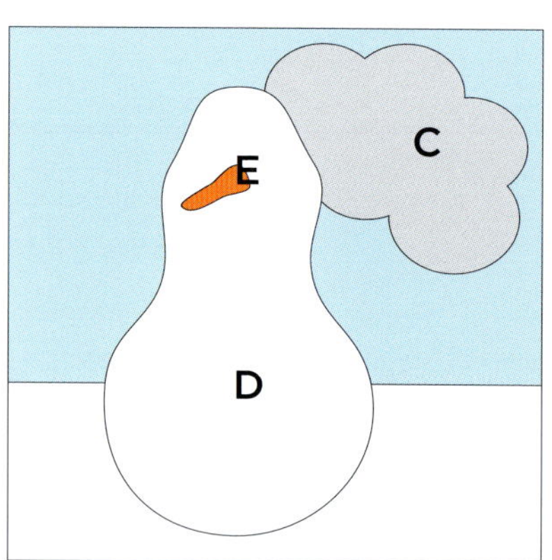

Embroidery

3. With two strands of floss and using a back stitch, embroider the arms and smile onto the snowman.

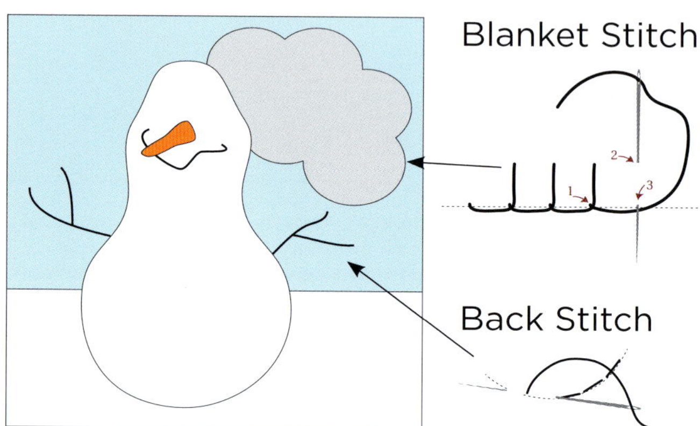

Optional: with two strands of embroidery floss, embroider the cloud with a blanket stitch.

4. Layer backing WS up, batting, and top WS down. Quilt. Bind with a ¼" seam allowance. *Hint:* it is helpful to baste ⅛" around the perimeter of the Itty Bitty Quilt before binding if quilting lightly.

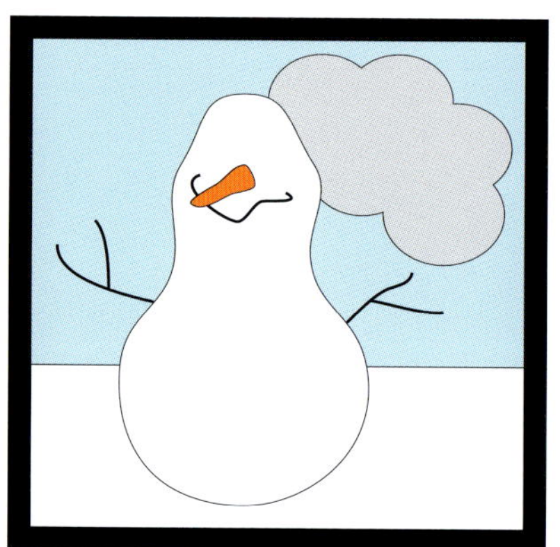

 Shown in Quilter's Candy Basics by Connecting Threads.

5. Sew button eyes and belly buttons to snowman.

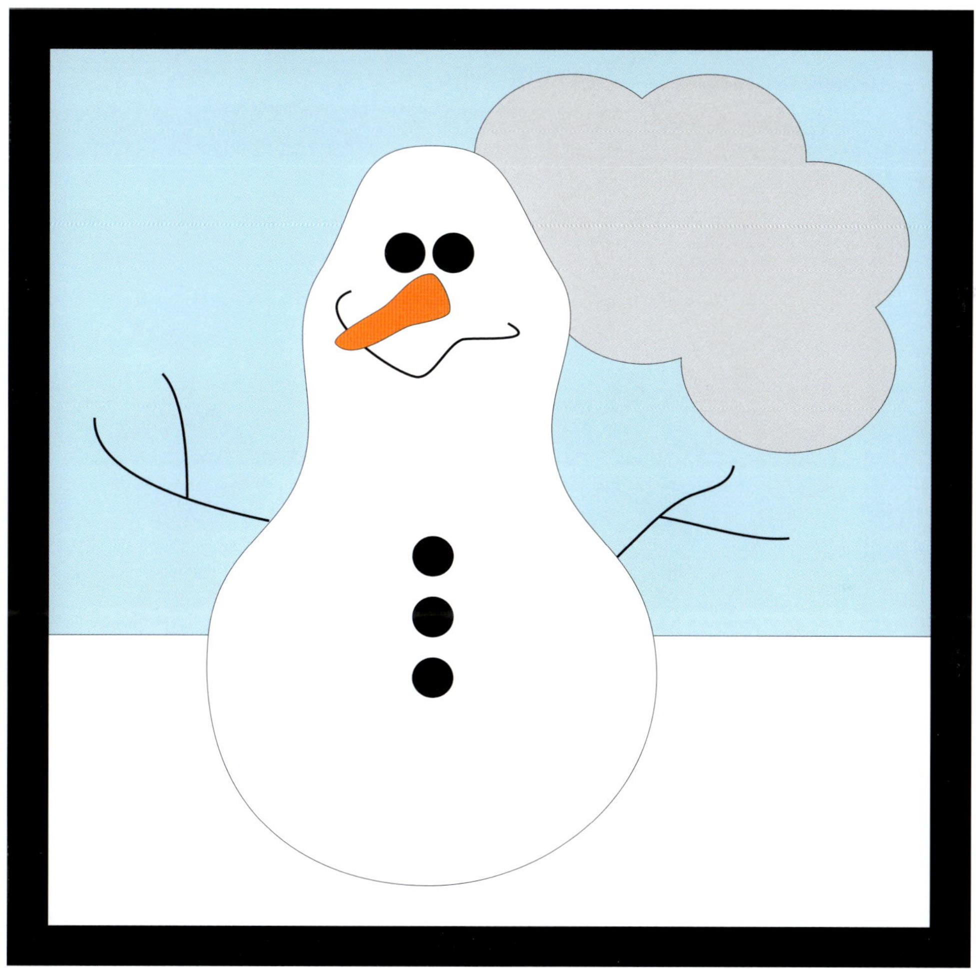

Itty Bitty February Heart

Approx. finished size: 6½″ square

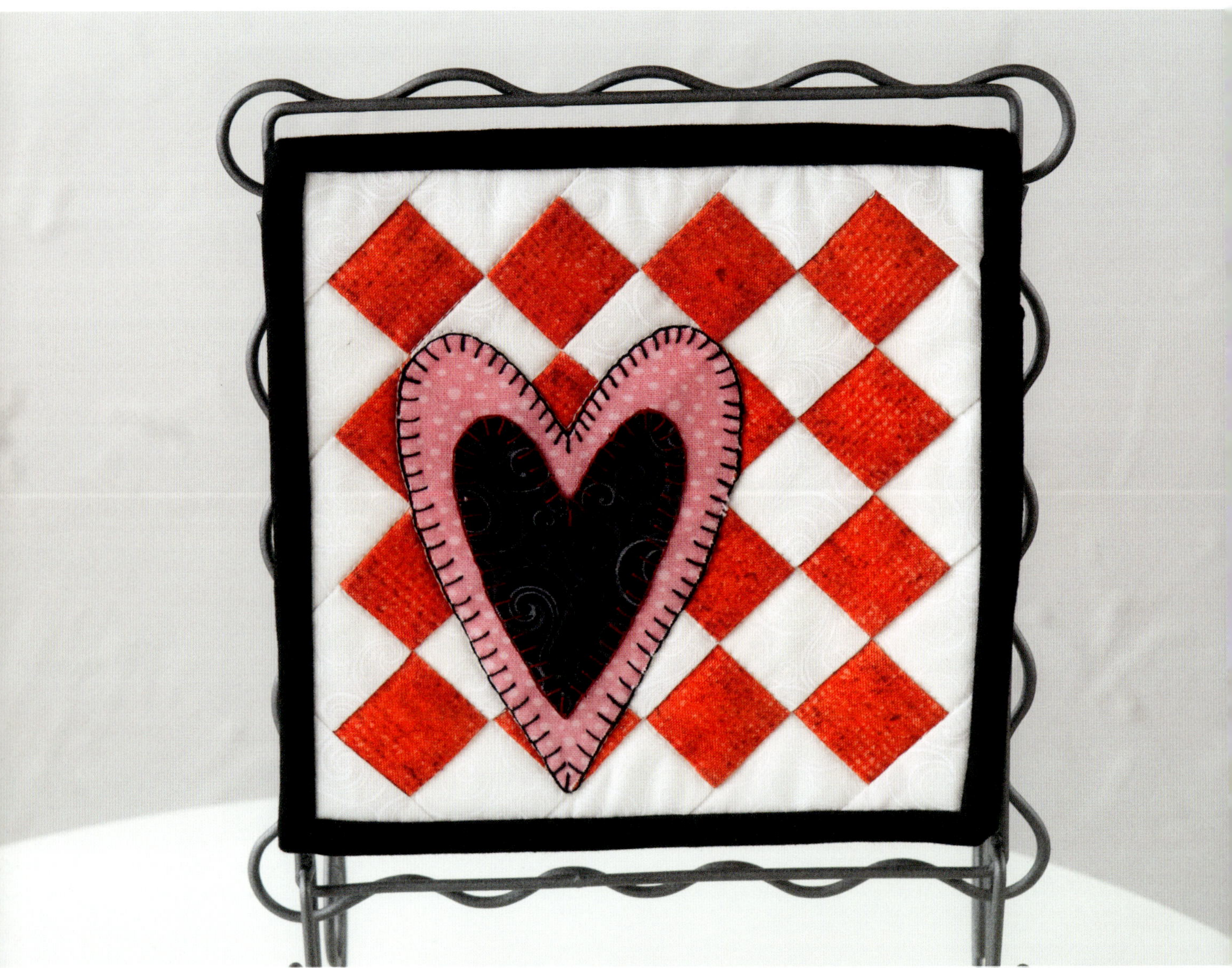

 Shown in Quilter's Candy Basics by Connecting Threads.

Connecting Threads Fabrics Used

- **Fabric 1:** Lotta Dots – Sweet Pink
- **Fabric 2:** Swirls – White on White
- **Fabric 3:** Faux Burlap – Cherry
- **Fabric 4:** Swirls – Black

Additional Supplies

- 21294 Lite Steam-A-Seam 2®
- Black and dark red embroidery thread
- Fusible woven interfacing (optional)

Please Note

Binding information for all Itty Bitty Quilts is on page 19.

Cutting suggestions are listed on pages 68 – 73.

Appliqué templates are listed on pages 74 – 78.

Cutting Instructions

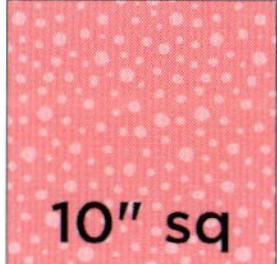

Fabric 1
A – One from template

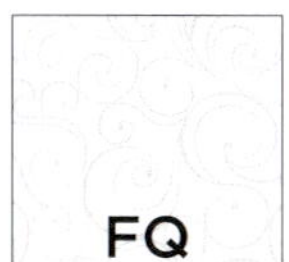

Fabric 2
B – Nine 1½″ squares
C – Three 4⅛″ squares
cut twice diagonally
D – Two 2⅞″ squares
cut once diagonally

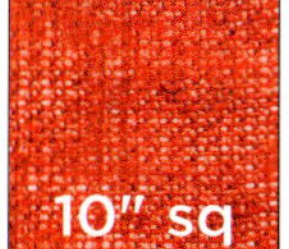

Fabric 3
E – Sixteen 1½″ squares

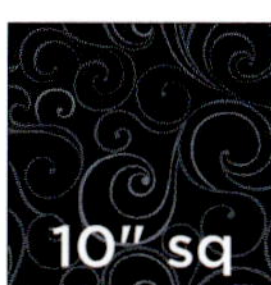

Fabric 4
F – One from template

Backing: An additional 9″ square

Directions

1. ***Row 1:*** Sew a **C** to facing sides of a **G** as shown. Press.

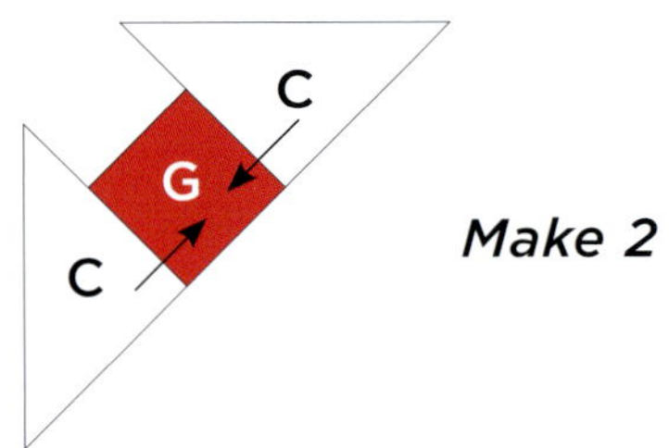

2. ***Row 2:*** Sew a **G** to facing sides of a **B**. Press. Sew a **C** to facing ends of the **G**/**B**/**G** unit. Press.

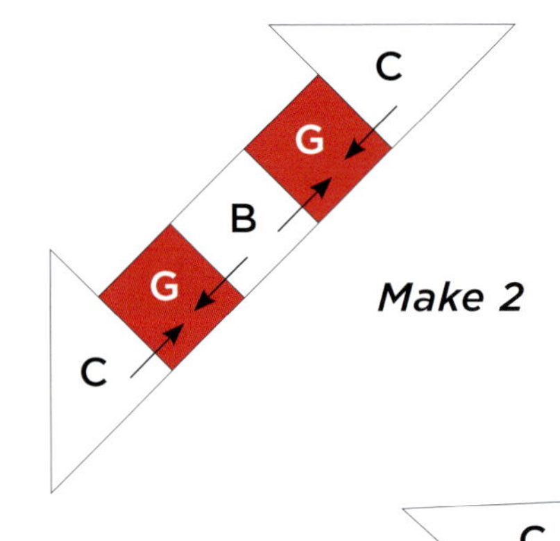

3. ***Row 3:*** Beginning with a **G**, alternate sewing three **G**s and two **B**s together. Press. Sew a **C** to facing ends. Press.

Make 2

4. ***Row 4:*** Beginning with a **G**, alternate sewing four **G**s and three **B**s together. Press. Make one.

5. Sew all rows together as shown. Trim. Press in one direction.

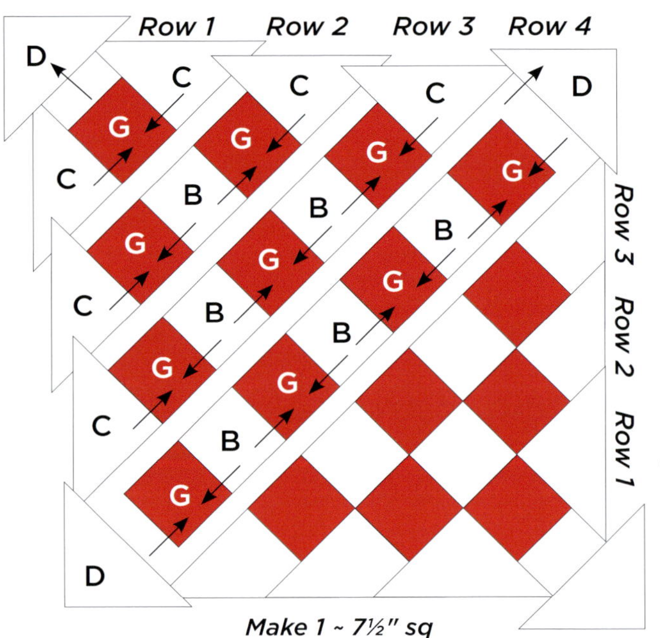

6. Sew on a **D** for each corner. Press.

7. Trim quilt to 6½" square.

8. With appliqué method of choice, appliqué in the following order: **A** and **F** to the Itty Bitty Quilt. *Hint:* adhere fusible woven interfacing onto back to hide embroidery stitches.

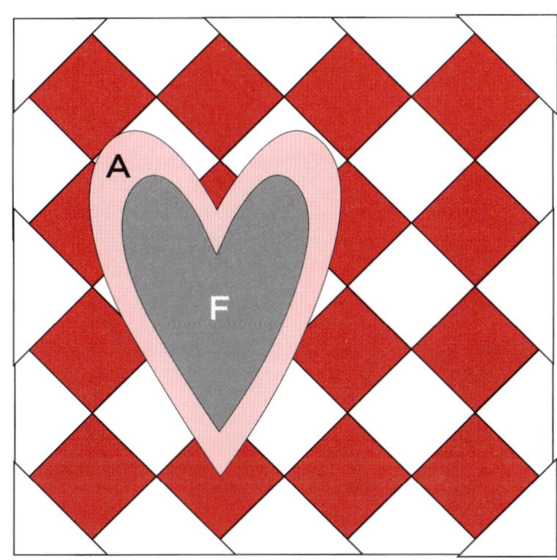

9. With two strands of black embroidery floss, embroider using a blanket stitch around **A**. Repeat with red floss around **F**.

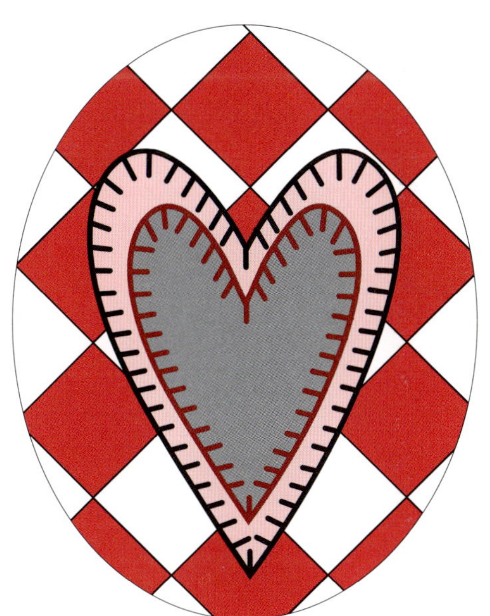

10. Layer backing WS up, batting, and top WS down. Quilt. Bind with a ¼″ seam allowance. *Hint:* it is helpful to baste around the perimeter of the Itty Bitty Quilt ⅛″ before binding if quilting lightly.

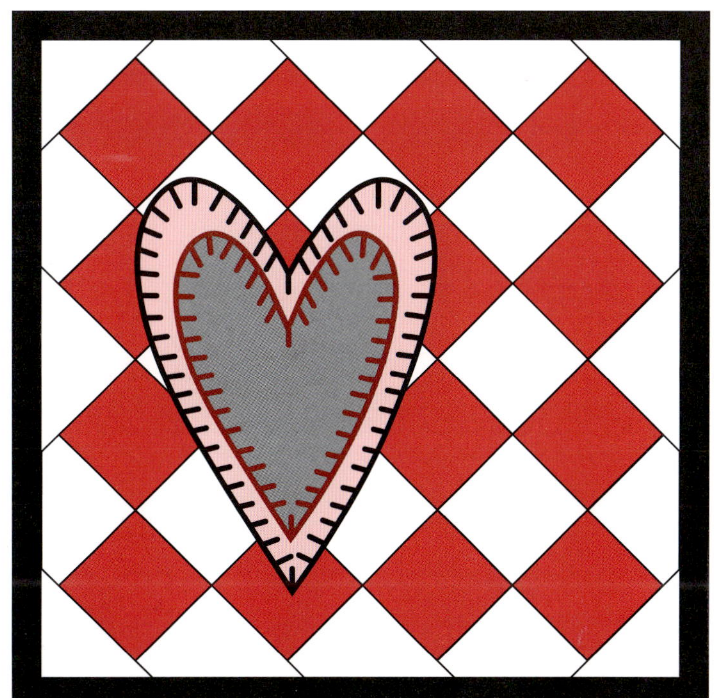

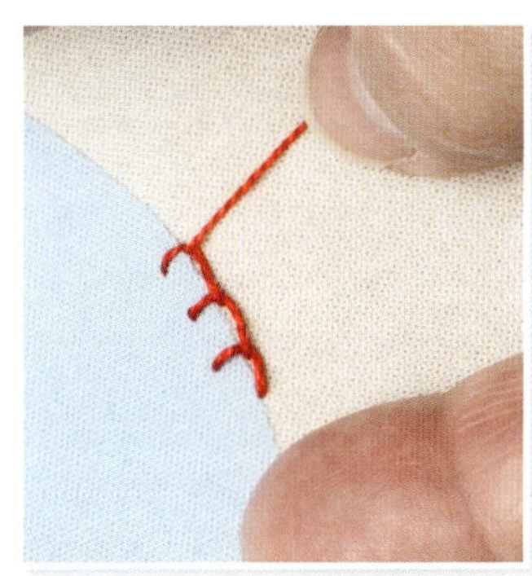

Blanket Stitch

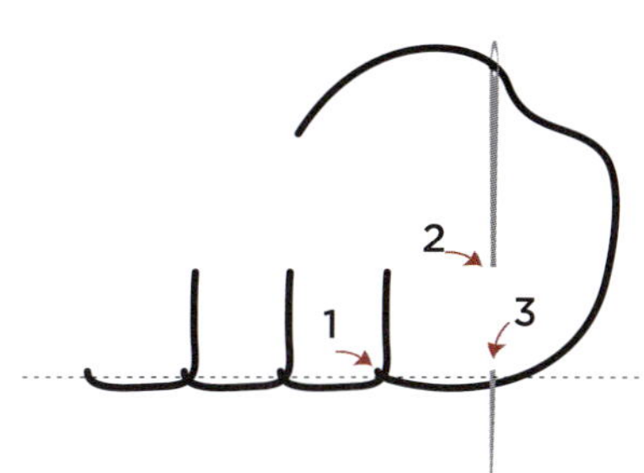

Itty Bitty March Daffodil

Approx. finished size: 6½″ square

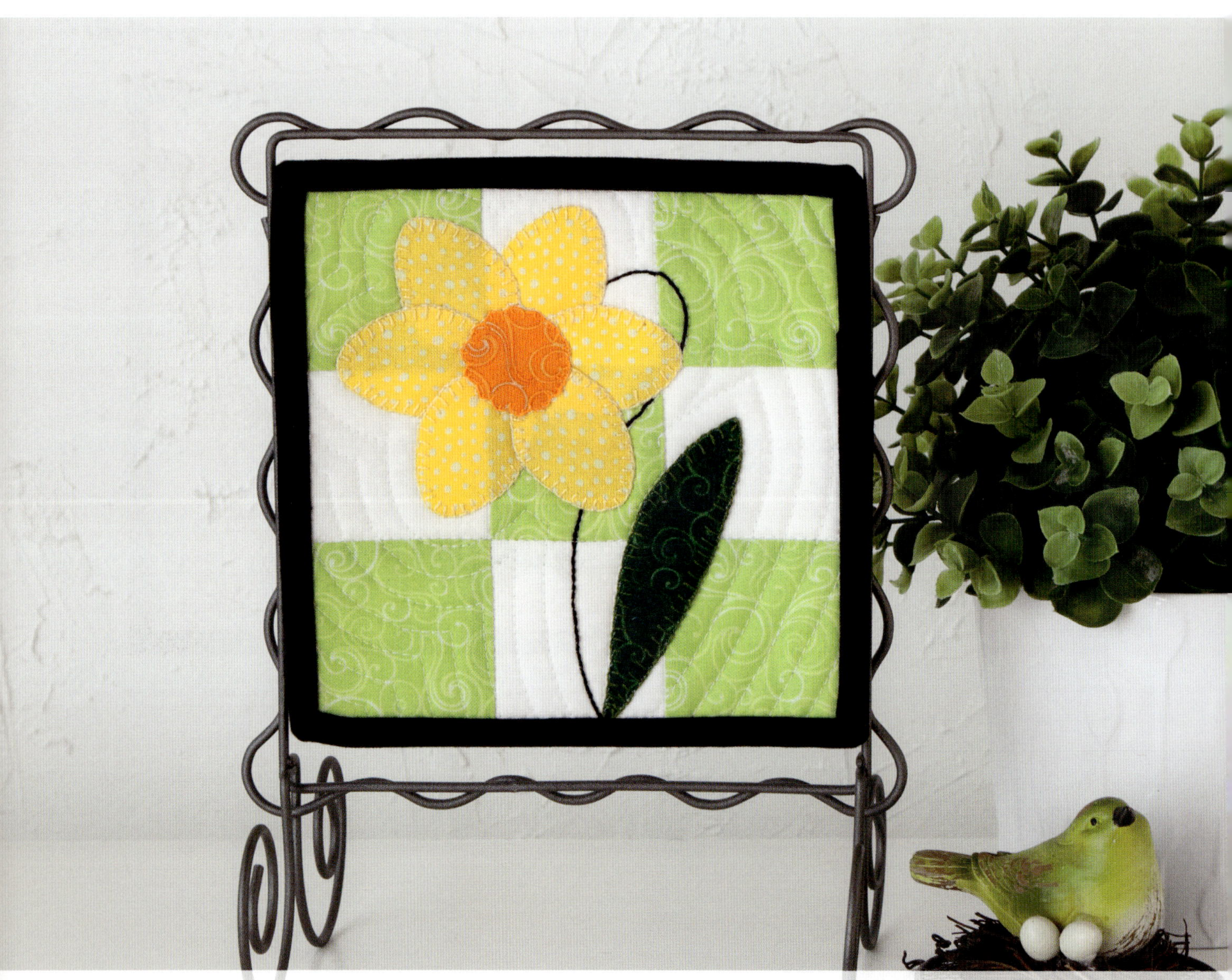

 Shown in Quilter's Candy Basics by Connecting Threads.

Connecting Threads Fabrics Used

- **Fabric 1:** Swirls - Lucid Pear
- **Fabric 2:** Lotta Dots - White on White
- **Fabric 3:** Lotta Dots - Sun
- **Fabric 4:** Swirls - Orange
- **Fabric 5:** Swirls - Ivy

Additional Supplies

- 21294 Lite Steam-A-Seam 2®
- Black embroidery floss
- Green, yellow, and orange embroidery floss (optional)
- Fusible woven interfacing (optional)

Please Note

Binding information for all Itty Bitty Quilts is on page 19.

Cutting suggestions are listed on pages 68 - 73.

Appliqué templates are listed on pages 74 - 78.

Cutting Instructions

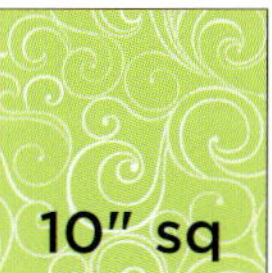

Fabric 1

A - Five 2½″ squares

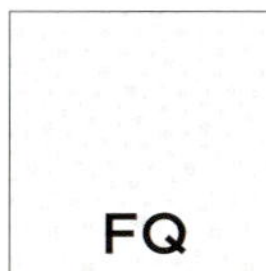

Fabric 2

B - Four 2½″ squares

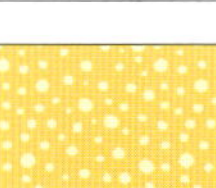

Fabric 3

C - Six from template

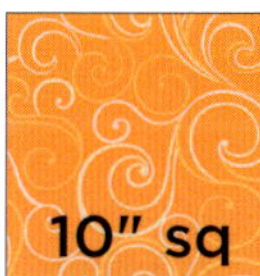

Fabric 4

D - One from template

Fabric 5

E - One from template

Backing: An additional 9″ square

Directions

1. Sew an **A** to facing sides of a **B**. Press.

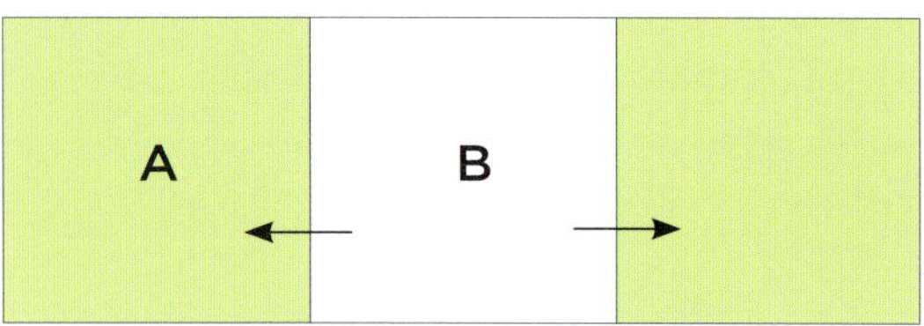

Make 2 ~ 2½" x 6½"

2. Sew a **B** to facing sides of an **A**. Press.

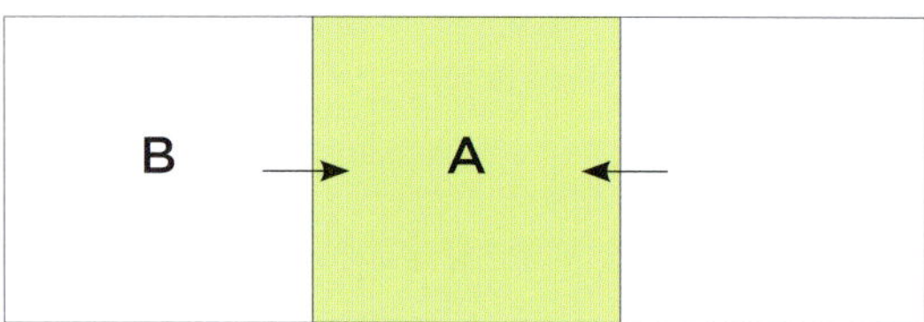

Make 1 ~ 2½" x 6½"

3. Sew a unit from Step 1 to facing sides of the unit from Step 2. Press.

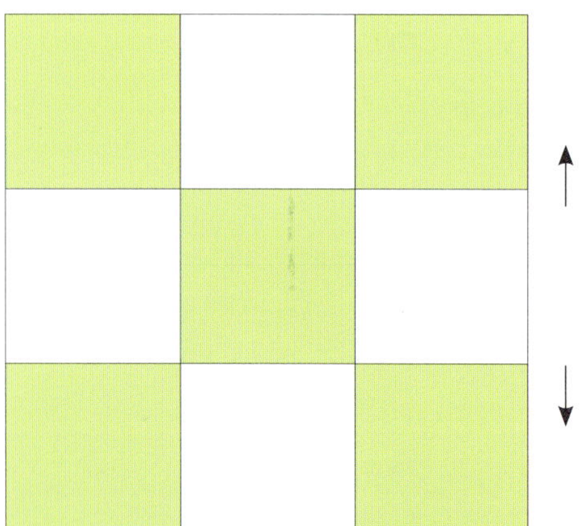

Embroidery

4. With three strands of black floss, embroider the stem onto the block with a stem stitch. *Hint:* adhere fusible woven interfacing onto back to hide embroidery stitches.

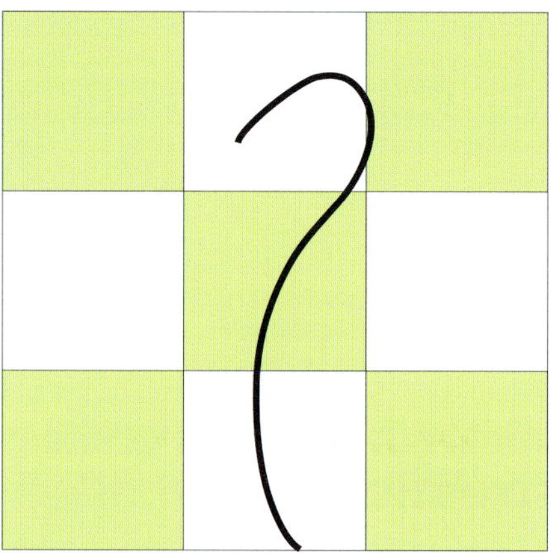

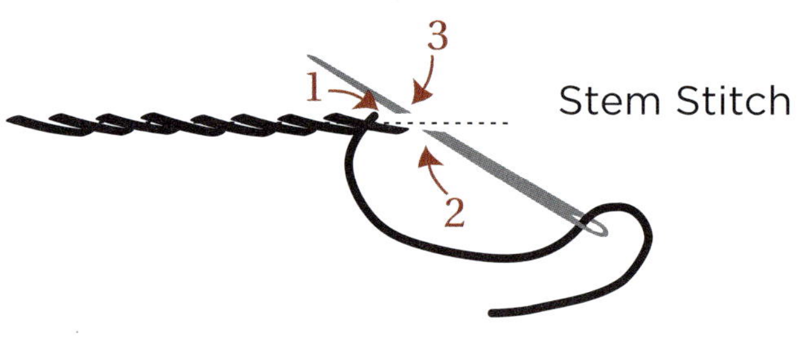

 Shown in Quilter's Candy Basics by Connecting Threads.

5. Using appliqué method of choice, appliqué **C** and **E** to the block.

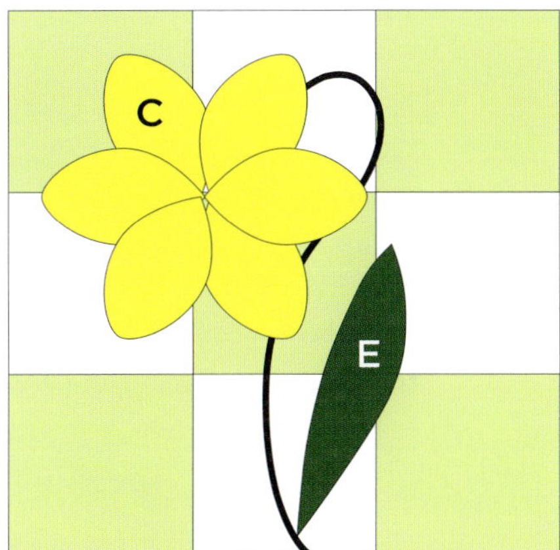

6. Appliqué **D** to the center of the daffodil.

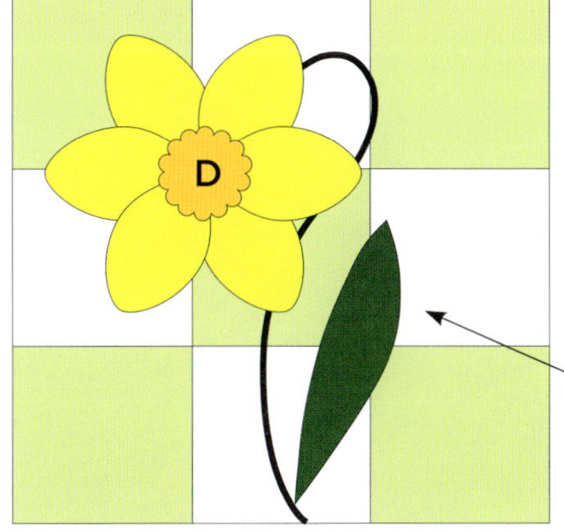

Optional: with two strands of embroidery floss, embroider the leaf, petals, and flower center with a blanket stitch.

7. Layer backing WS up, batting, and top WS down. Quilt. Bind with a ¼″ seam allowance. *Hint:* it is helpful to baste around the perimeter of the Itty Bitty Quilt ⅛″ before binding if quilting lightly.

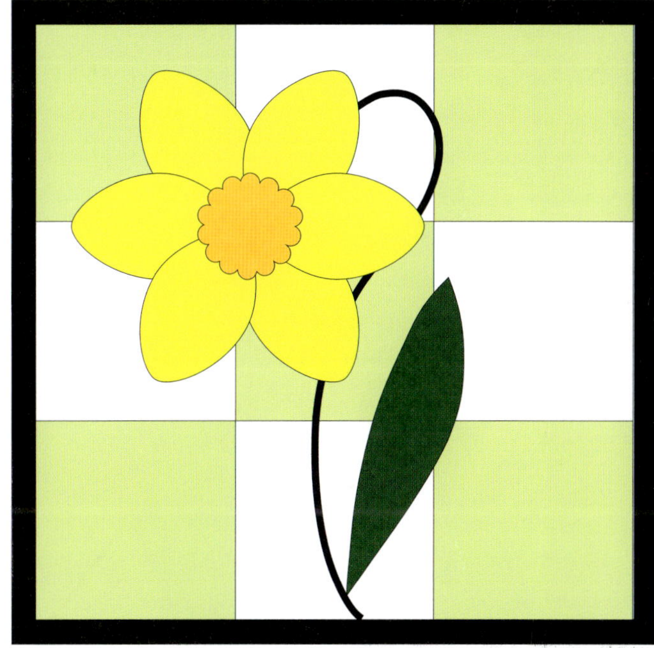

Itty Bitty April Showers

Approx. finished size: 6½" square

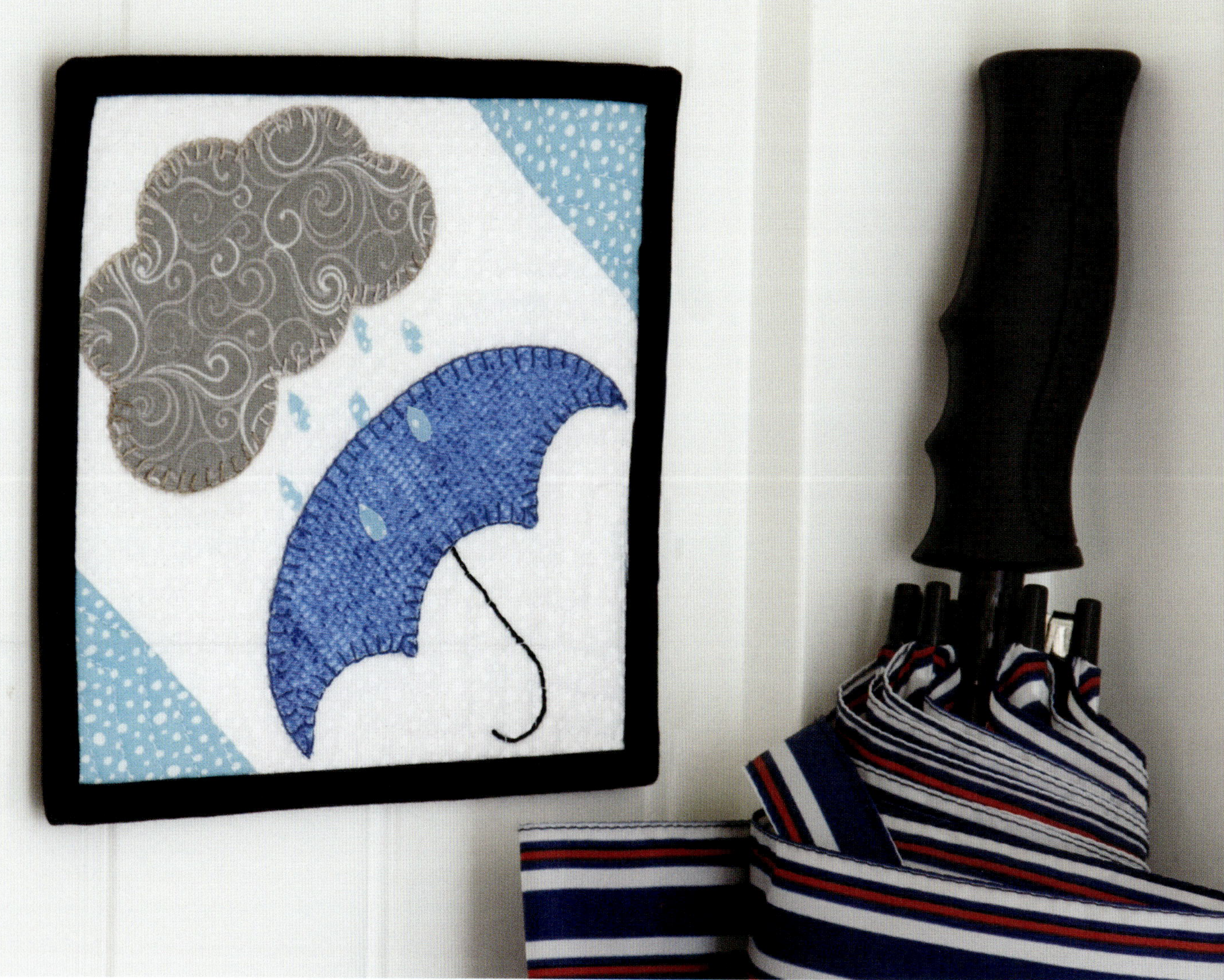

 Shown in Quilter's Candy Basics by Connecting Threads.

Connecting Threads Fabrics Used

- **Fabric 1:** Lotta Dots - Ocean Mist
- **Fabric 2:** Lotta Dots - White on White
- **Fabric 3:** Faux Burlap - Bluebird
- **Fabric 4:** Swirls - Stone

Additional Supplies

- 21294 Lite Steam-A-Seam 2®
- Black embroidery floss
- Grey and blue embroidery floss (optional)
- Fusible woven interfacing (optional)

Please Note

Binding information for all Itty Bitty Quilts is on page 19.

Cutting suggestions are listed on pages 68 - 73.

Appliqué templates are listed on pages 74 - 78.

Cutting Instructions

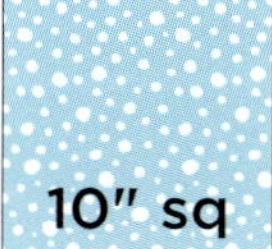

Fabric 1

A - Two 2½″ squares marked once diagonally

B - Seven from template (or embroider)

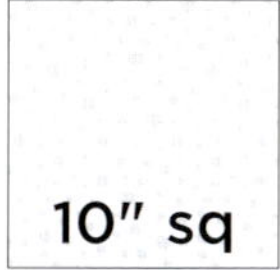

Fabric 2

C - One 6½″ square

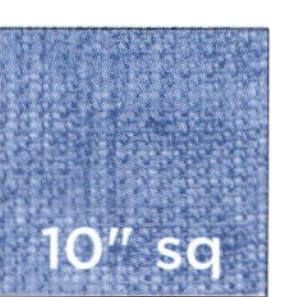

Fabric 3

D – One from template

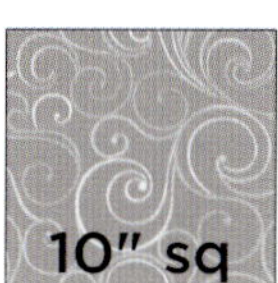

Fabric 4

E - One from template

Backing: An additional 9″ square

Directions

1. Lay an **A** in opposite, diagonal corners of **C**. Sew along the marked line. Cut corner off, leaving a ¼" seam allowance. Press. *Hint:* adhere fusible woven interfacing onto back to hide embroidery stitches.

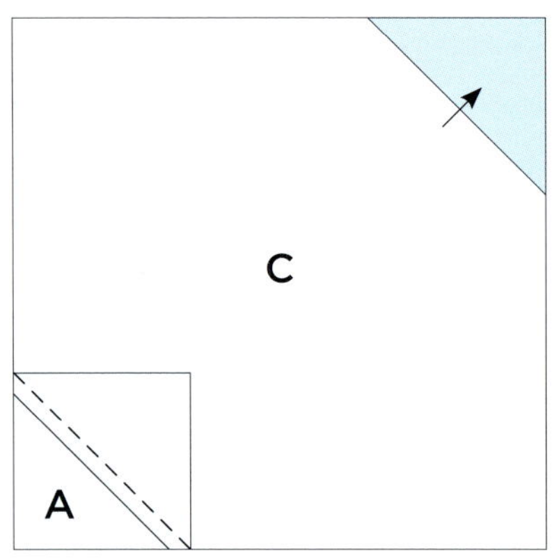

Make 1
6½" square

Appliqué

2. Position and appliqué in the following order, **D**, **E**, and **B**s on the **A**/**C** unit. *Hint:* another option for creating **B** is with embroidery.

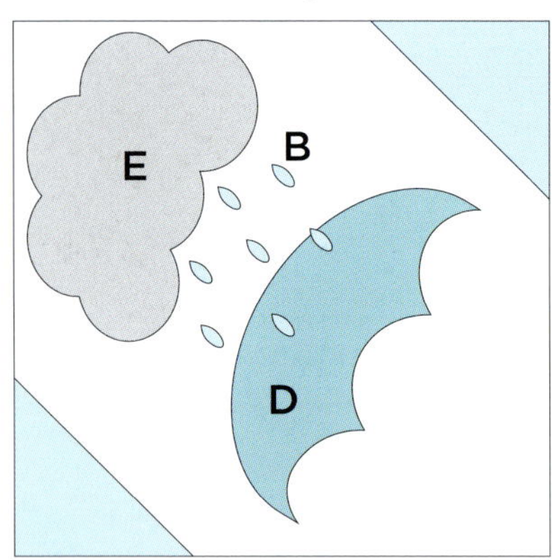

Embroidery

3. With three strands of floss, embroider the umbrella handle using a stem stitch.

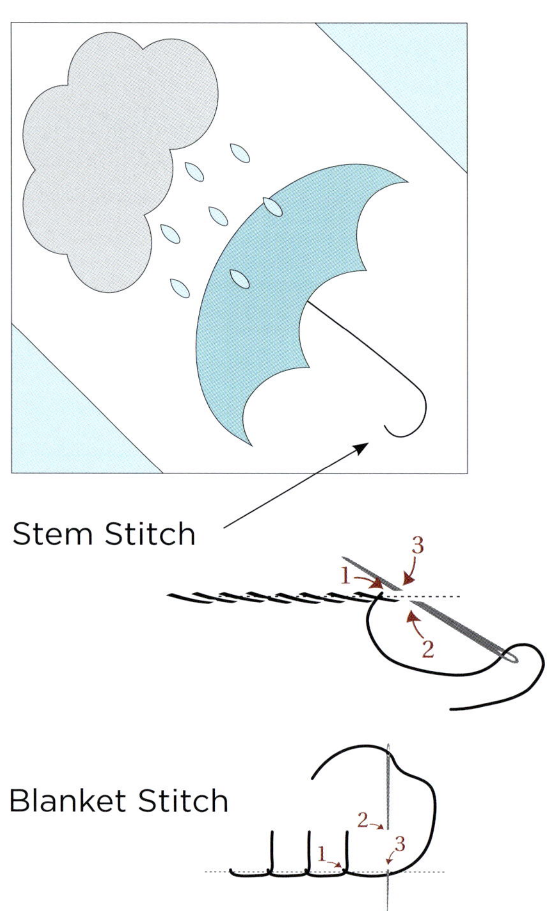

Optional: with two strands of embroidery floss, embroider the cloud and umbrella with a blanket stitch.

 Shown in Quilter's Candy Basics by Connecting Threads.

4. Layer backing WS up, batting, and top WS down. Quilt. Bind with a ¼″ seam allowance. *Hint:* it is helpful to baste around the perimeter of the Itty Bitty Quilt ⅛″ before binding if quilting lightly.

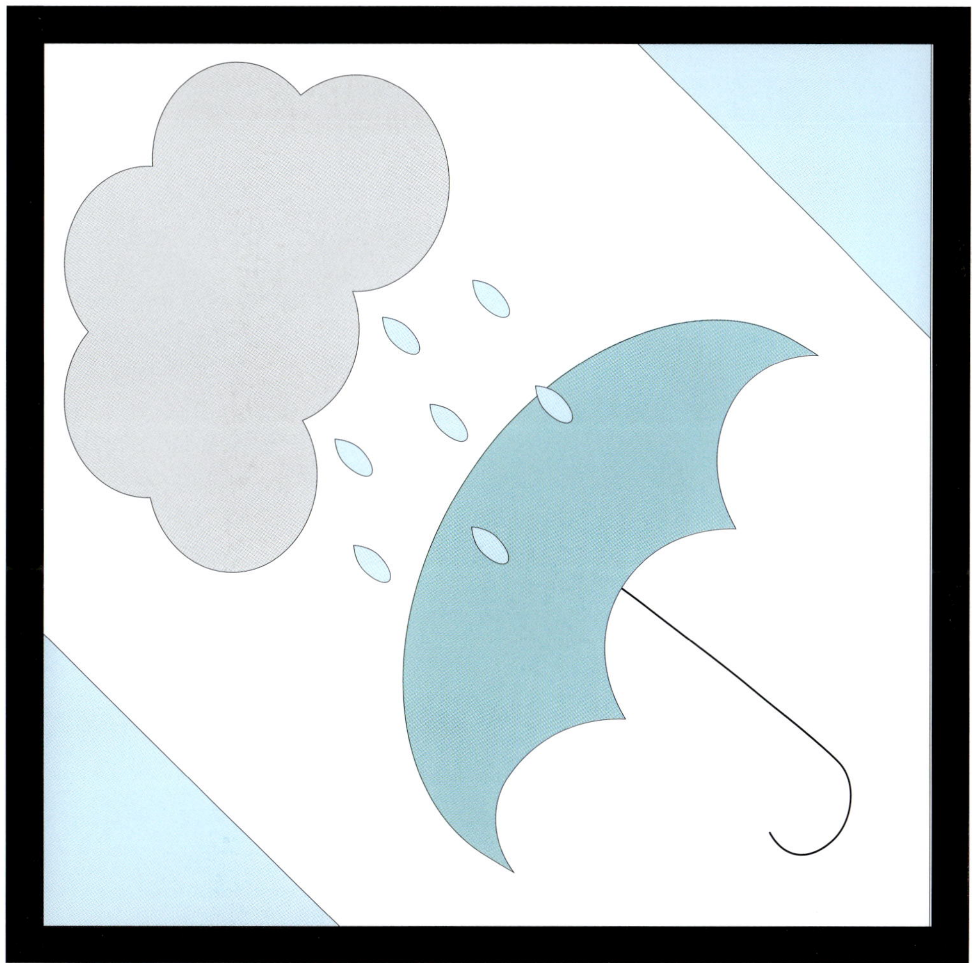

Itty Bitty May Flowers

Approx. finished size: 6½″ square

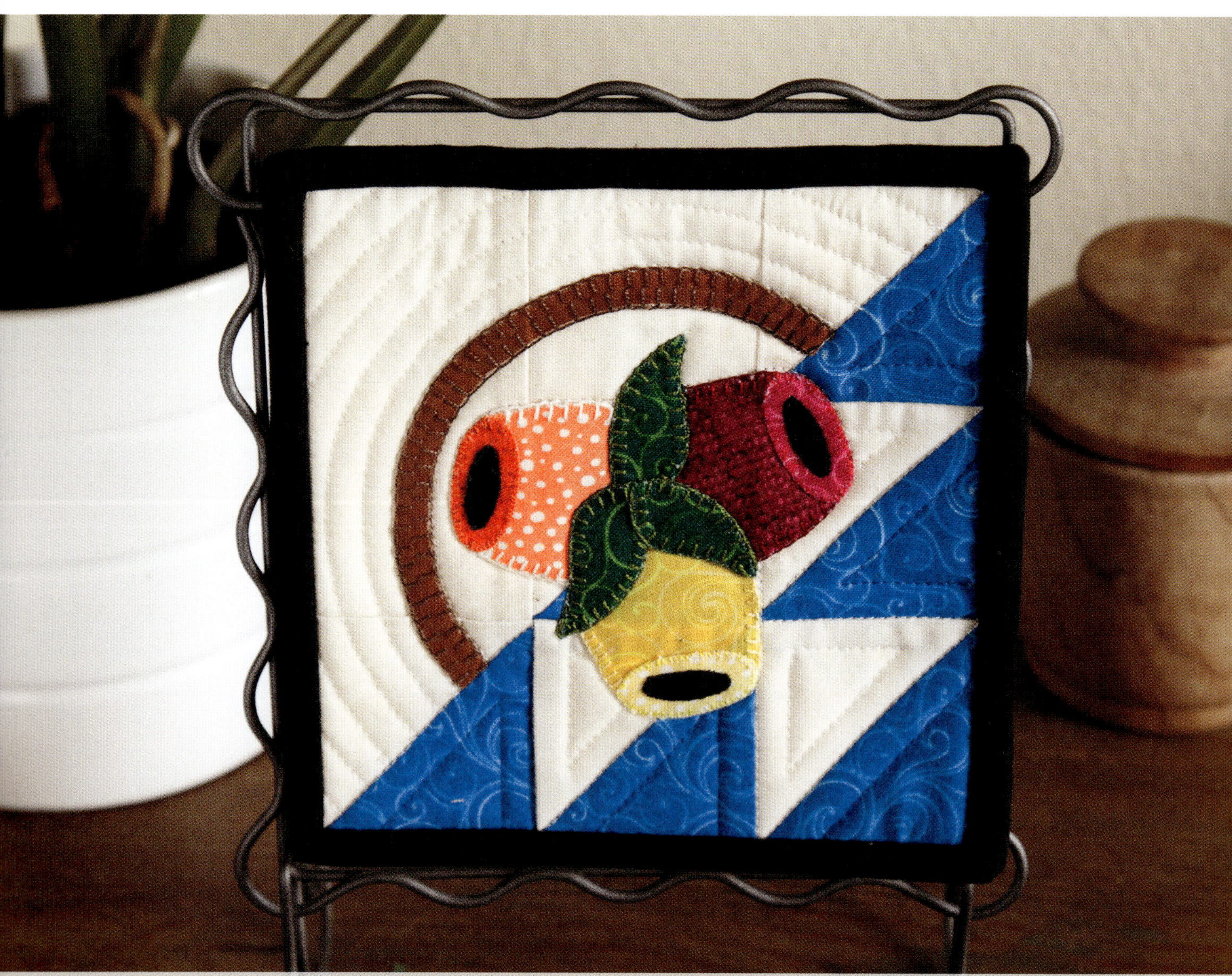

 Shown in Quilter's Candy Basics by Connecting Threads.

Connecting Threads Fabrics Used

- **Fabric 1:** Mirage – Cream
- **Fabric 2:** Swirls – Imperial Blue
- **Fabric 3:** Lotta Dots – Melon
- **Fabric 4:** Faux Burlap – Cherry
- **Fabric 5:** Swirls – Marigold
- **Fabric 6:** Lotta Dots – Honeysuckle
- **Fabric 7:** Faux Burlap – Beet Red
- **Fabric 8:** Swirls – Sangria
- **Fabric 9:** Swirls – Ivy
- **Fabric 10:** Solid – Curry
- **Fabric 11:** Solid – Black

Additional Supplies

- 21294 Lite Steam-A-Seam 2®
- Brown, white, dark violet, fuchsia, yellow, green, and coral embroidery floss (optional)
- Fusible woven interfacing (optional)

Please Note

Binding information for all Itty Bitty Quilts is on page 19.

Cutting suggestions are listed on pages 68 – 73.

Appliqué templates are listed on pages 74 – 78.

Cutting Instructions

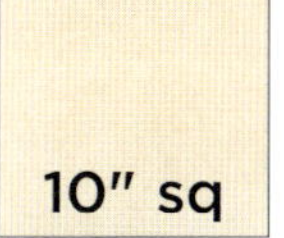

Fabric 1
A – Three 2⅞″ squares
B – One 2½″ square
C – One 2½″ x 4½″

Fabric 2
D – Three 2⅞″ squares

Fabric 3
E – One from template

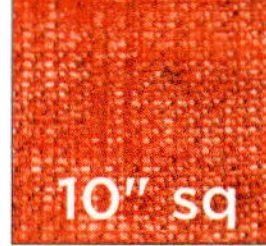

Fabric 4
F – One from template

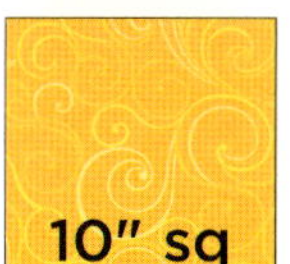

Fabric 5
E – One from template

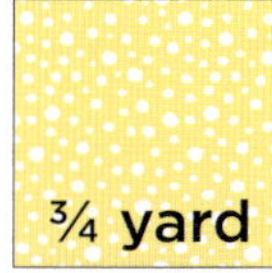

Fabric 6
F – One from template

Fabric 7
E – One from template

Fabric 8
F – One from template

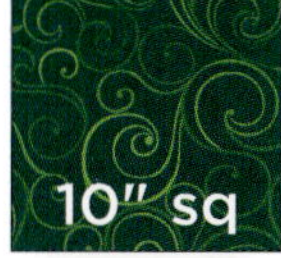

Fabric 9
G – Three from template, two reversed.

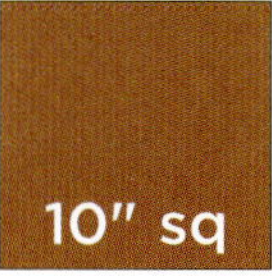

Fabric 10
H – One from template

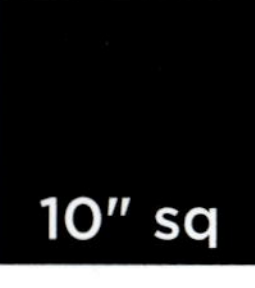

Fabric 11
J – Three from template

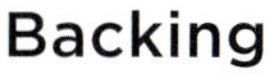

Backing
An additional 9″ square

Directions

1. Draw a diagonal line through all **A**s. Draw a line ¼" on each side of the center diagonal line. Layer an **A** and a **D** together. Stitch slightly to the center of the ¼" line and cut on the center line. Press.

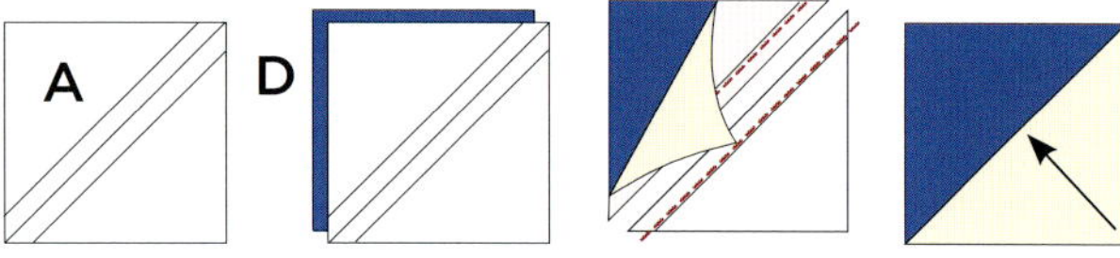

Make 6 ~ 2½" square

2. Sew two **A/D** units together. Press. Sew an **A/D** unit and **B** together. Press. Sew the double **A/D** unit to the **A/D/B** unit together. Press. Sew **C** to this unit as shown. Press.

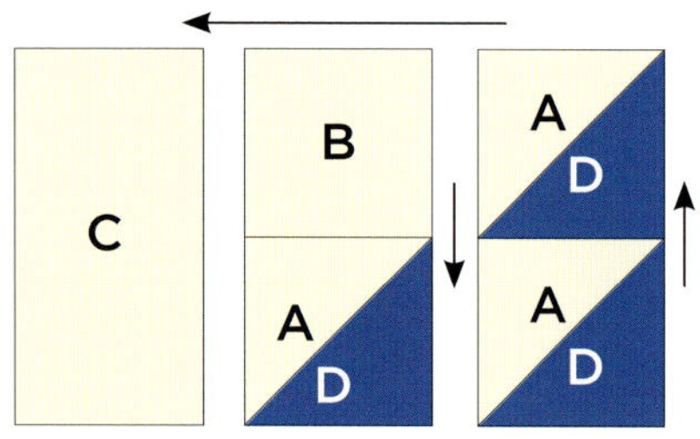

Make 1 ~ 4½" x 6½"

3. Sew the three remaining **A/D** units together as shown. Press. Sew the triple **A/D** unit to the bottom of the unit from Step 2. Press.

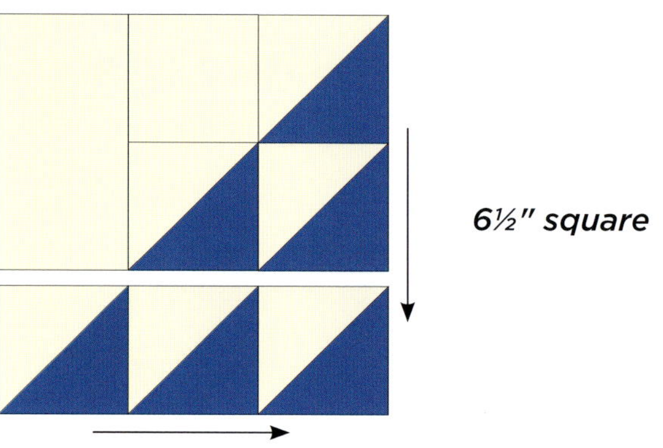

6½" square

Appliqué

4. Using appliqué method of choice, appliqué **H** to the quilt.

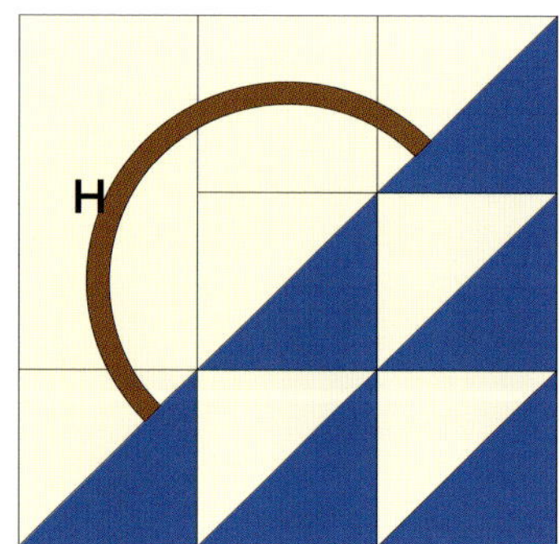

5. Appliqué in the following order all **E**s, **F**s, **G**s, and **J**s to the quilt.

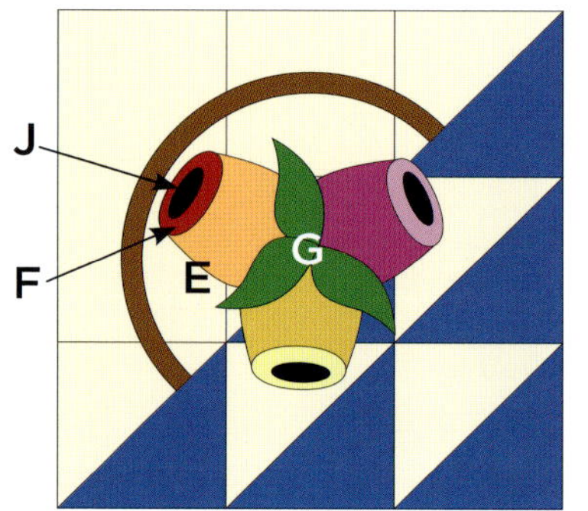

Optional: with one strand of embroidery floss, embroider **J** & **F** with a stem stitch, **E** & **G** and the handle with two strands and using a blanket stitch.

 Shown in Quilter's Candy Basics by Connecting Threads.

6. Layer backing WS up, batting, and top WS down. Quilt. Bind with a ¼″ seam allowance. *Hint:* it is helpful to baste around the perimeter of the Itty Bitty Quilt ⅛″ before binding if quilting lightly.

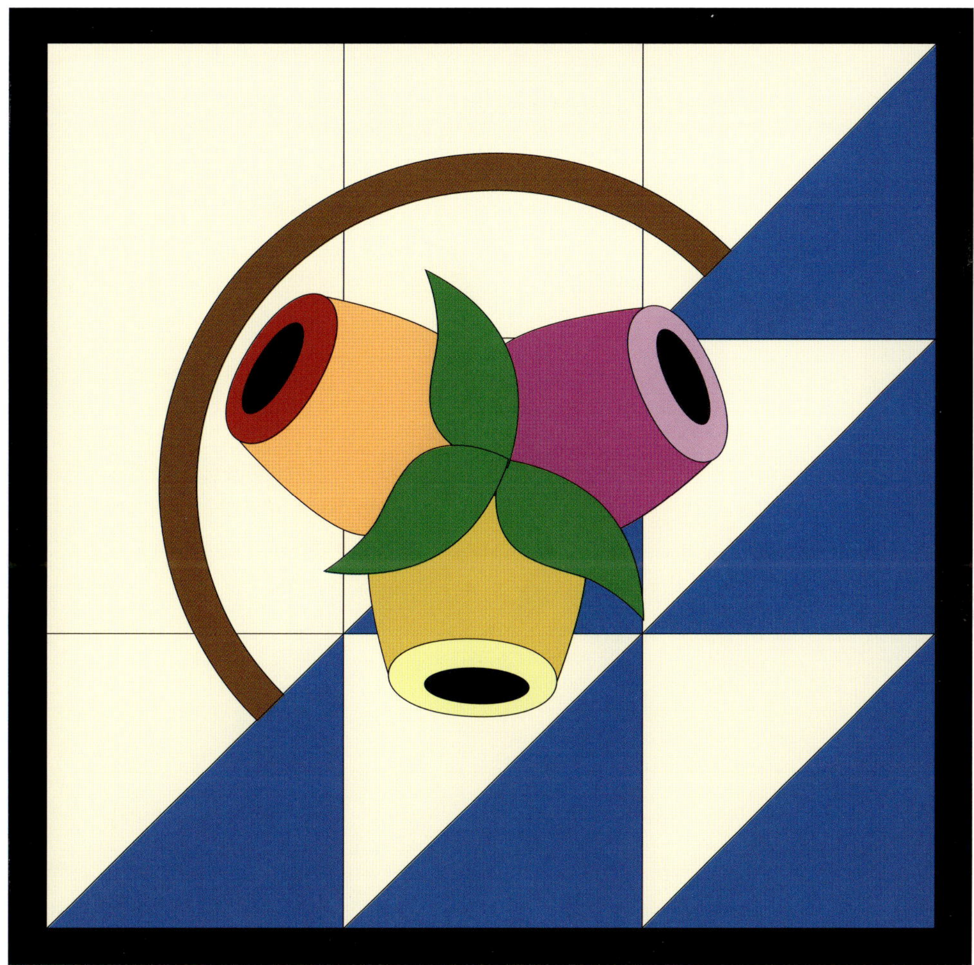

Itty Bitty June Watermelon

Approx. finished size: 6½" square

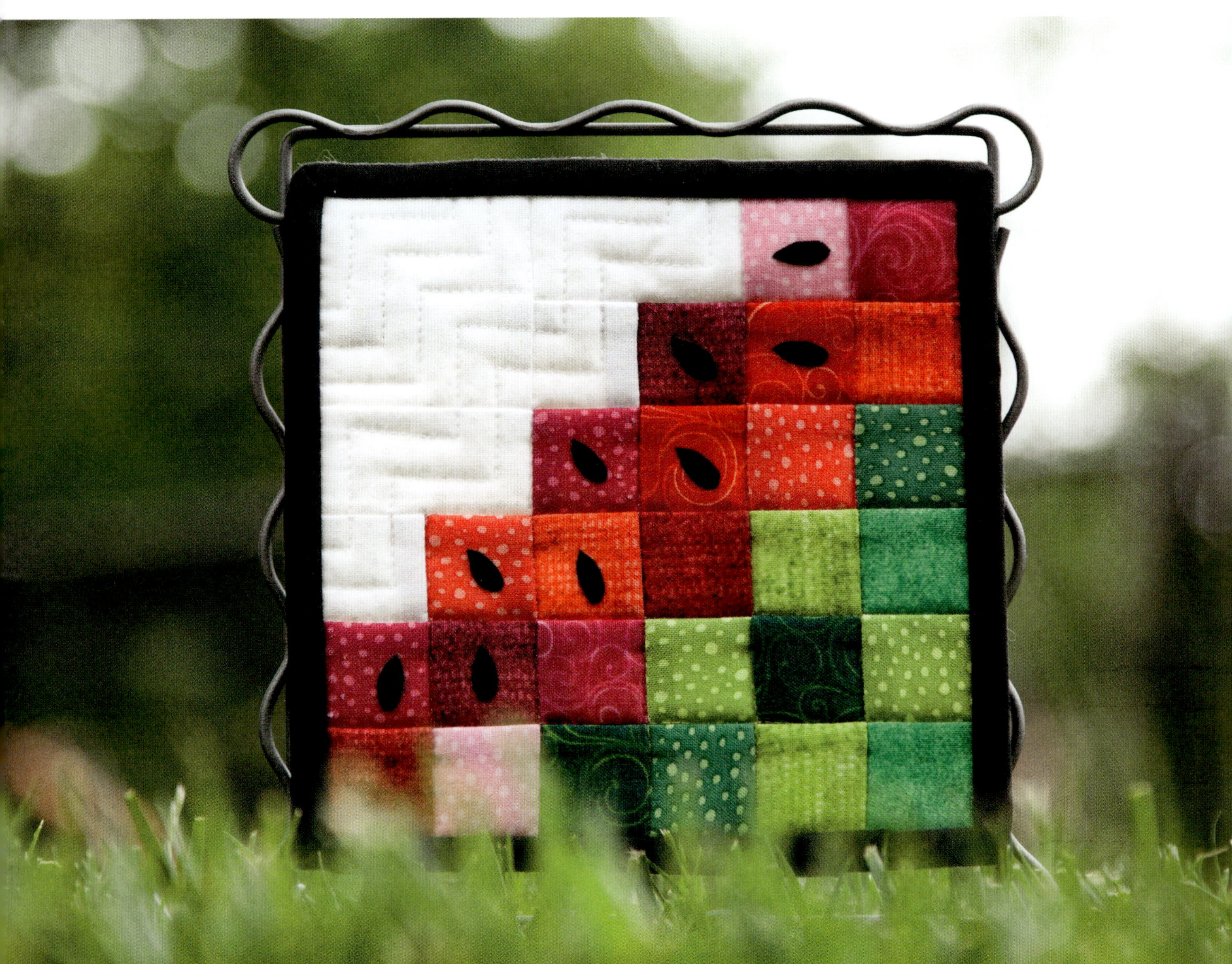

 Shown in Quilter's Candy Basics by Connecting Threads.

Connecting Threads Fabrics Used

- **Fabric 1:** Lotta Dot - White on White
- **Fabric 2:** Swirls - Sangria
- **Fabric 3:** Swirls - Red
- **Fabric 4:** Lotta Dot - Sweet Pink
- **Fabric 5:** Faux Burlap - Cherry
- **Fabric 6:** Faux Burlap - Merlot
- **Fabric 7:** Lotta Dot - Tomato
- **Fabric 8:** Lotta Dot - Sangria
- **Fabric 9:** Faux Burlap - Beet Red
- **Fabric 10:** Lotta Dot - Amazon
- **Fabric 11:** Faux Burlap - Lime
- **Fabric 12:** Mirage - Shamrock
- **Fabric 13:** Lotta Dot - Lime
- **Fabric 14:** Swirls - Ivy
- **Fabric 15:** Solid - Black

Additional Supplies

- 21294 Lite Steam-A-Seam 2®
- (9) ¼" buttons (optional)
- Black embroidery floss (optional)
- Fusible woven interfacing (optional)

Please Note

Binding information for all Itty Bitty Quilts is on page 19.

Cutting suggestions are listed on pages 68 - 73.

Appliqué templates are listed on pages 74 - 78.

Cutting Instructions

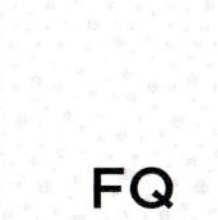

Fabric 1

A - One 2½" square
B - Two 1½" squares
C - Two 1½" x 2½"

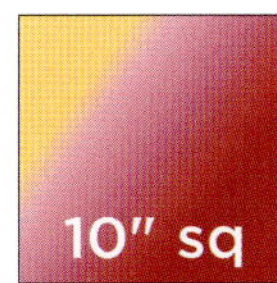

Fabrics 2-14

D - Two 1½" squares

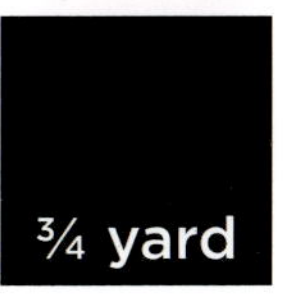

Fabric 15

E - Nine from template (optional)

Backing: An additional 9" square

Directions

Hint: it might be helpful to arrange the pieces ahead of time to achieve a design configuration pleasing to you.

1. Sew two different **D**s from Fabrics 2-9 together. Press. Sew a **C** to the left end as shown. Press.

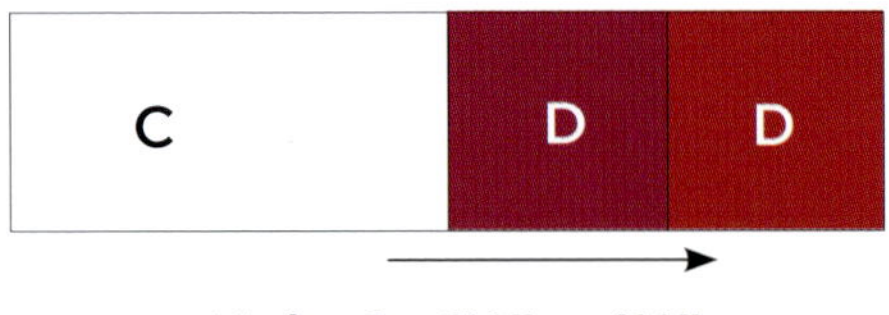

Make 1 ~ 1½" x 4½"

2. Sew three different **D**s from Fabrics 2-9 together. Press. Sew a **B** to the left end as shown. Press.

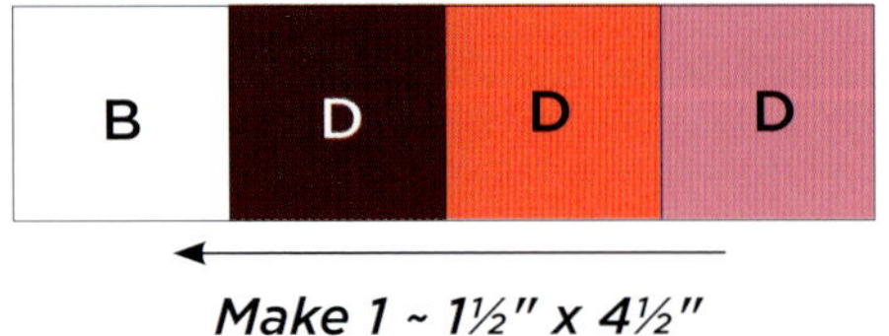

Make 1 ~ 1½" x 4½"

3. Sew the unit from Step 1 to the unit from Step 2 as shown. Press. Sew **A** to the left end as shown. Press.

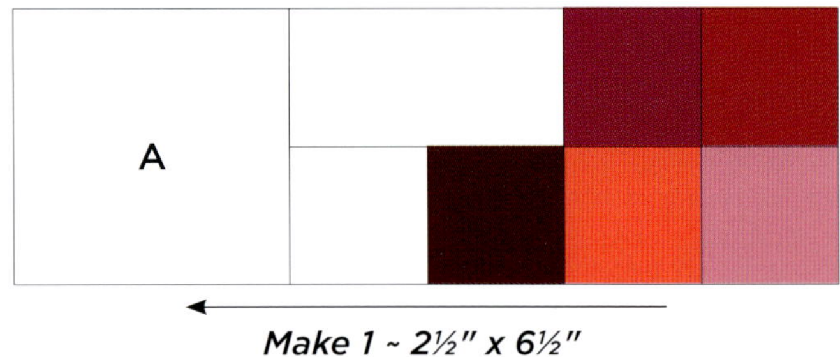

Make 1 ~ 2½" x 6½"

4. Sew three different **D**s from Fabrics 2-9 together. Press. Sew one **D** from Fabrics 10-14 to the right end as shown. Press. Sew a **C** to the left end as shown. Press.

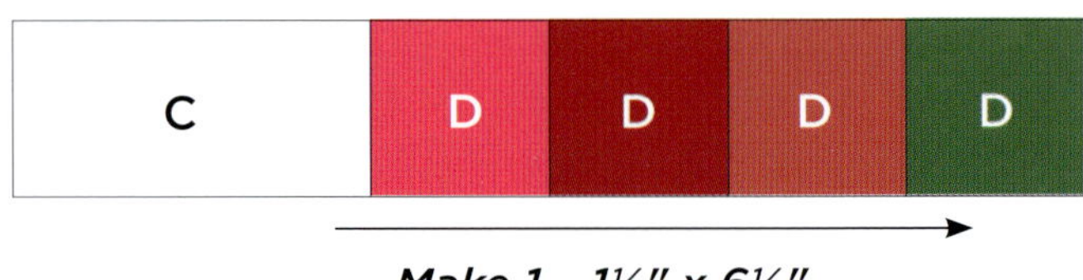

Make 1 ~ 1½" x 6½"

5. Sew three different **D**s from Fabrics 2-9 together. Press. Sew two different **D**s from Fabrics 10-14 to the right end as shown. Press. Sew a **B** to the left end as shown. Press.

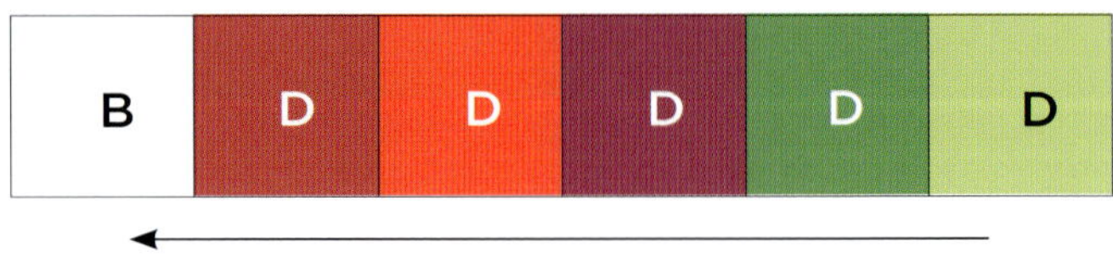

Make 1 ~ 1½" x 6½"

6. Sew three different **D**s from Fabrics 2-9 together. Press. Sew three different **D**s from Fabrics 10-14 to the right end as shown. Press.

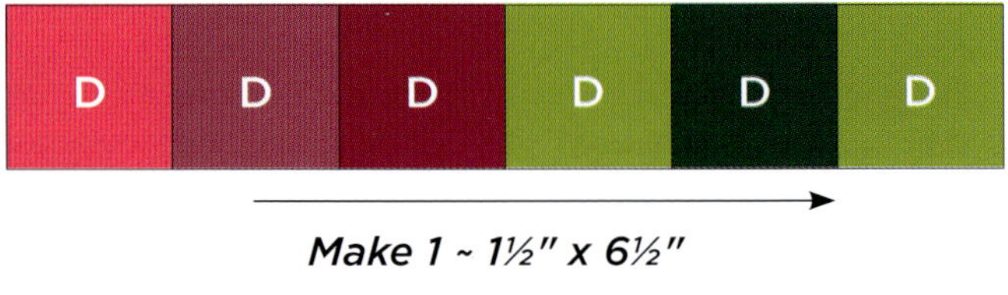

Make 1 ~ 1½" x 6½"

 Shown in Quilter's Candy Basics by Connecting Threads.

7. Sew two different **D**s from Fabrics 2-9 together. Press. Sew four **D**s from Fabrics 10-14 to the right end as shown. Press.

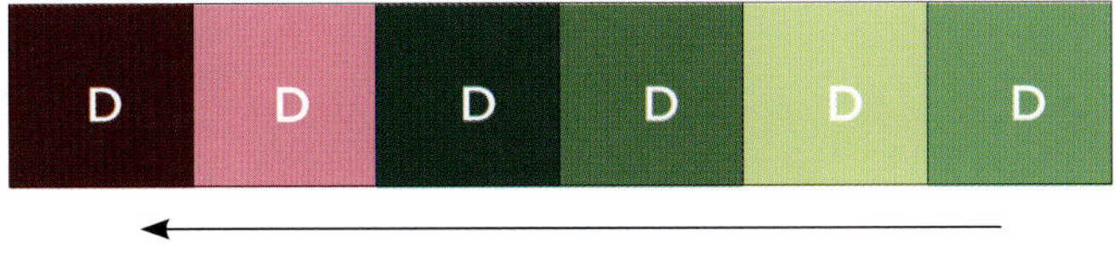

Make 1 ~ 1½" x 6½"

8. Sew all rows from Steps 3-7 together. Press.

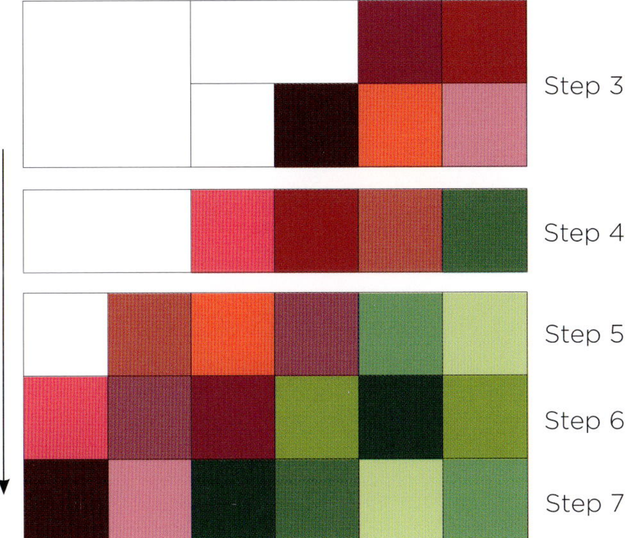

6½" square

Appliqué

9. Using appliqué method of choice, appliqué all **E**s to the quilt. *Hint:* the seeds can also be created with embroidery using three strands of floss and a satin stitch, or, attach buttons. Should you choose to embroider it is helpful to adhere fusible woven interfacing onto back to hide embroidery stitches.

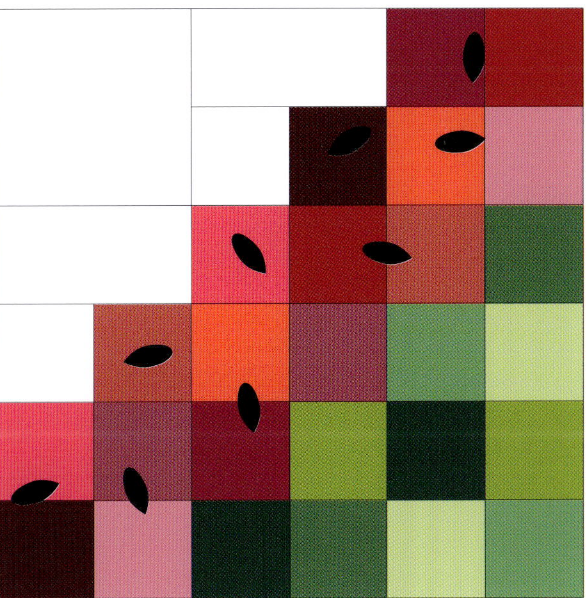

Satin Stitch

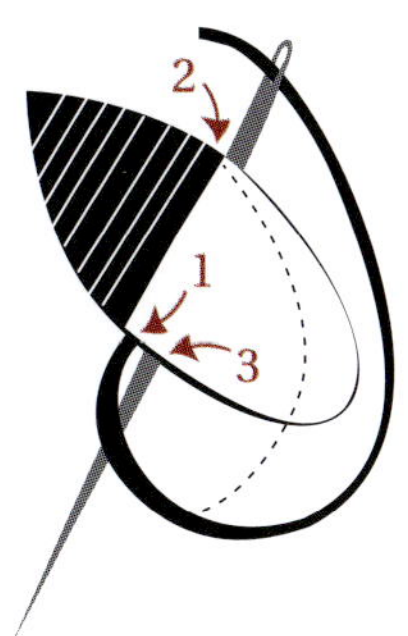

10. Layer backing WS up, batting, and top WS down. Quilt. Bind with a ¼″ seam allowance. *Hint:* it is helpful to baste around the perimeter of the Itty Bitty Quilt ⅛″ before binding if quilting lightly.

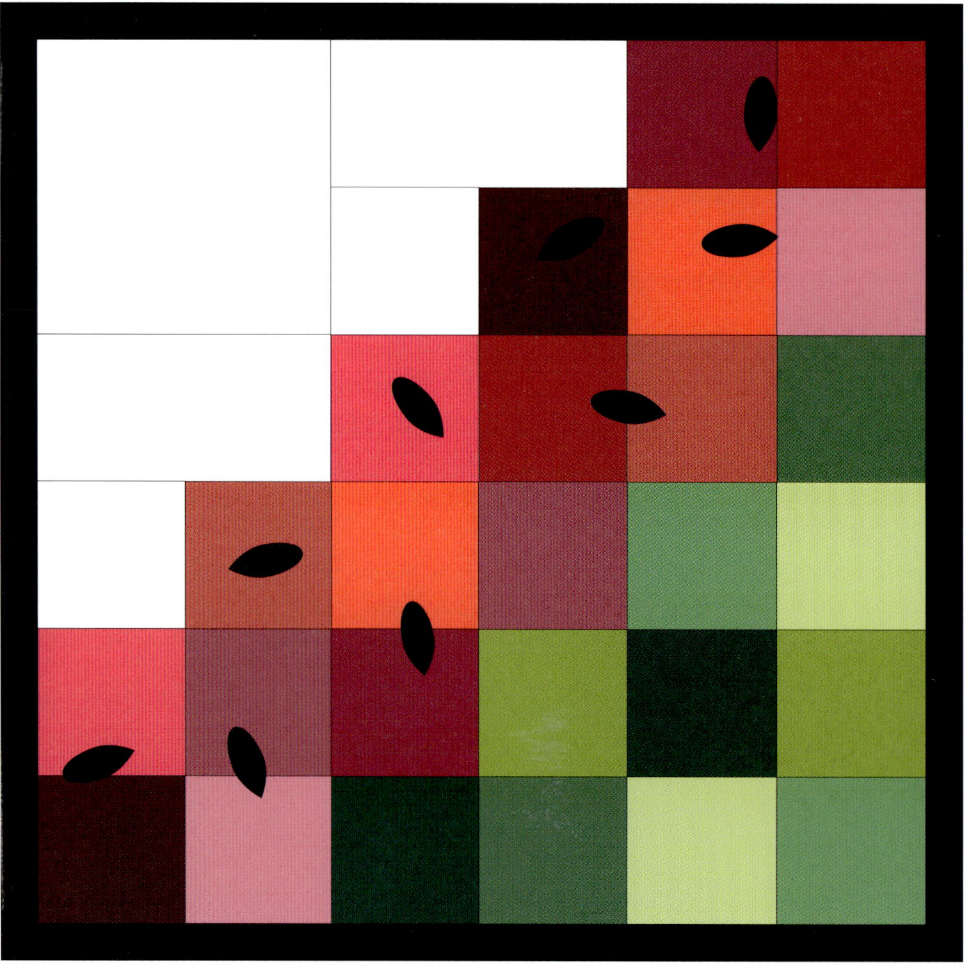

 Shown in Quilter's Candy Basics by Connecting Threads.

Bonus! Other great *Itty Bitty Quilt* layout ideas:

1. Use three blocks together to create a mini table runner.

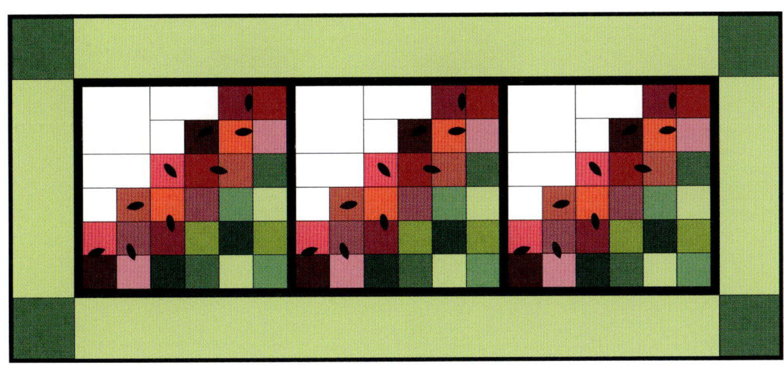

2. Take one block and turn it into a trivet or pot holder.

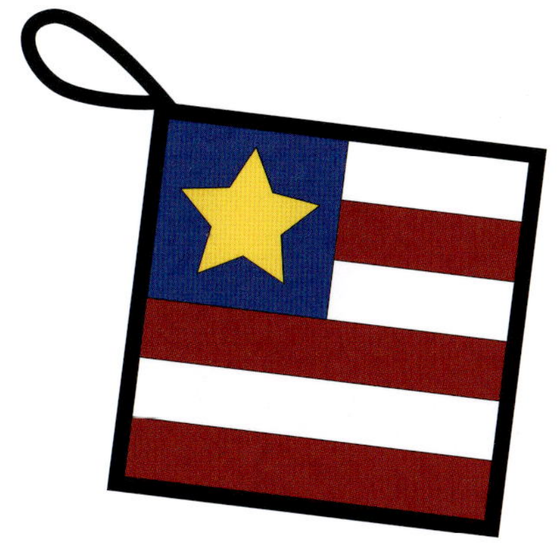

3. Use four blocks to make a pillow.

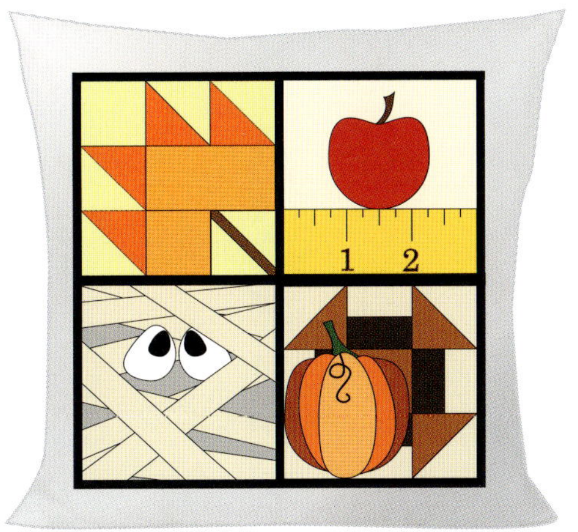

Itty Bitty July Flag

Approx. finished size: 6½" square

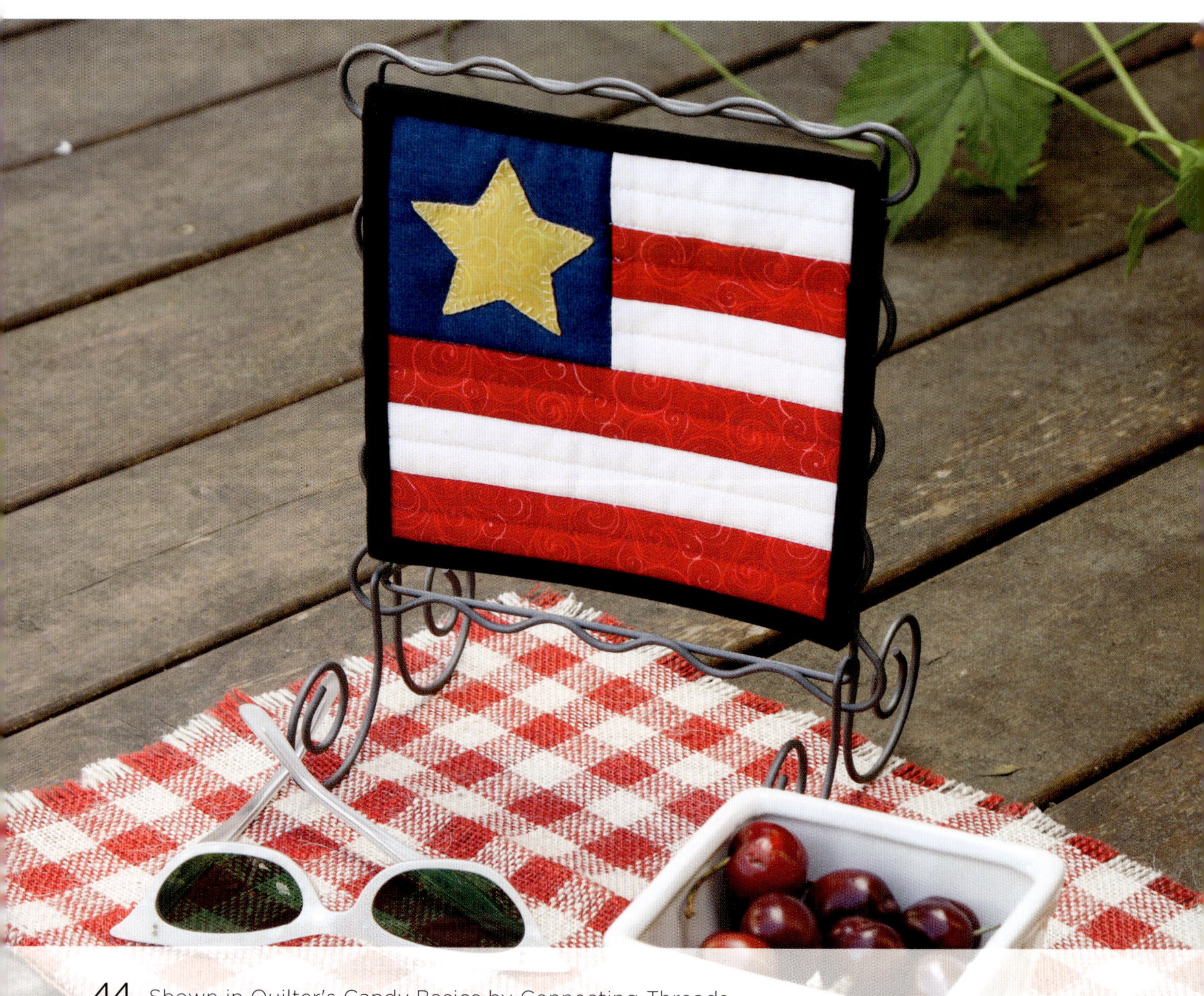

 Shown in Quilter's Candy Basics by Connecting Threads.

Connecting Threads Fabrics Used

- **Fabric 1:** Lotta Dots – White on White
- **Fabric 2:** Swirls – Marigold
- **Fabric 3:** Mirage – Patriot Blue
- **Fabric 4:** Swirls – Red

Additional Supplies

- 21294 Lite Steam-A-Seam 2®
- Gold embroidery floss (optional)
- Fusible woven interfacing (optional)

Please Note

Binding information for all Itty Bitty Quilts is on page 19.

Cutting suggestions are listed on pages 68 – 73.

Appliqué templates are listed on pages 74 – 78.

Cutting Instructions

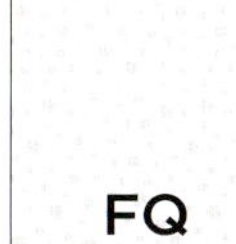

Fabric 1

A - One 1½″ x 6½″
B - Two 1½″ x 3½″

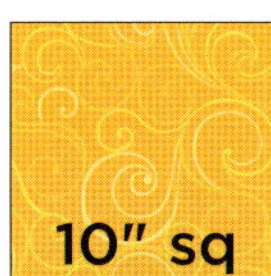

Fabric 2

C – One from template

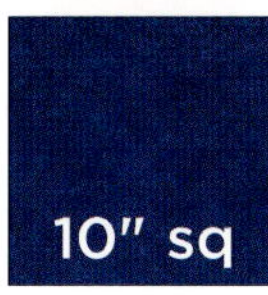

Fabric 3

D – One 3½″ square

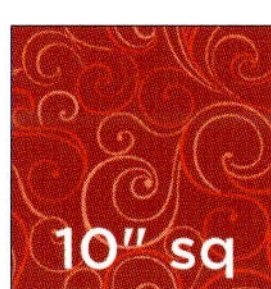

Fabric 4

E - Two 1½″ x 6½″
F - One 1½″ x 3½″

Backing: An additional 9″ square

Directions

Appliqué

1. Using appliqué method of choice, appliqué **C** to **D**.

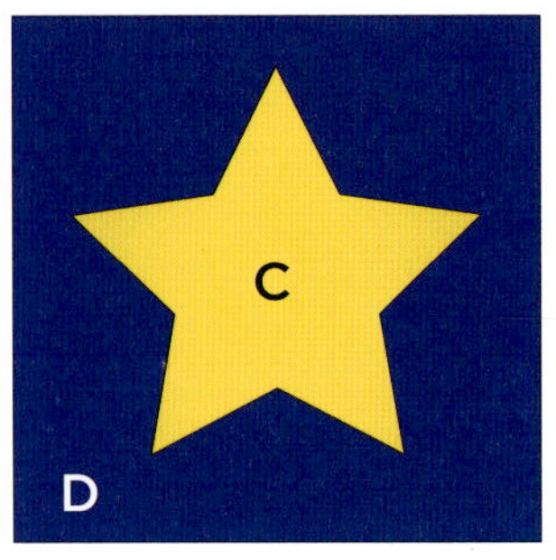

Make 1 ~ 3½" square

2. Sew a **B** to facing sides of an **F**. Press.

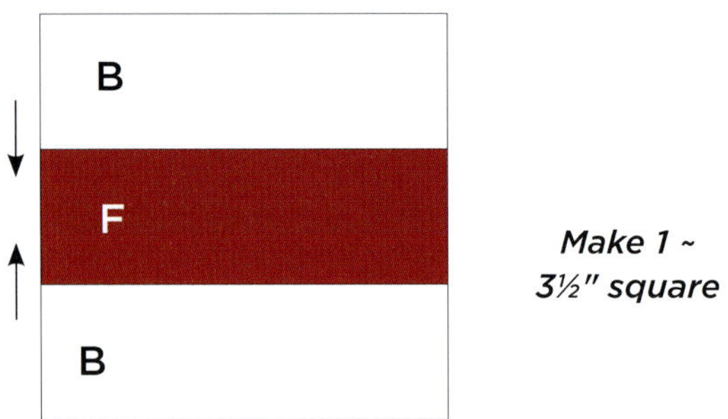

Make 1 ~ 3½" square

3. Sew the **C**/**D** unit to the left side of the **B**/**F**/**B** unit. Press.

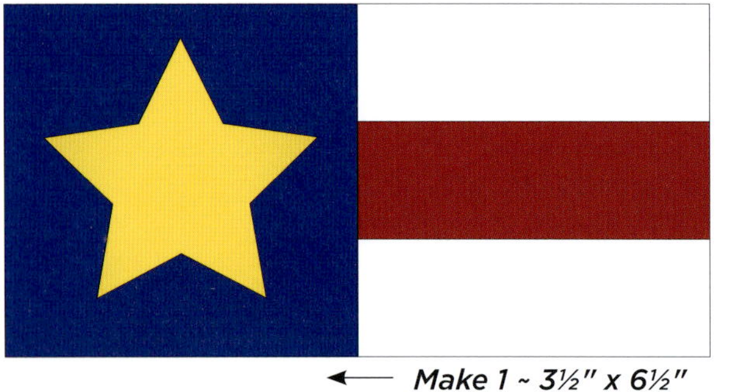

Make 1 ~ 3½" x 6½"

4. Sew an **E** to facing sides of an **A**. Press.

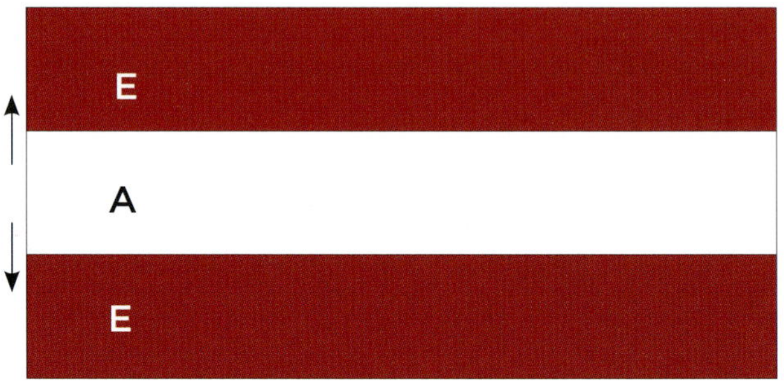

Make 1 ~ 3½" x 6½"

5. Sew the unit from Step 3 to the unit from Step 4 as shown. Press.

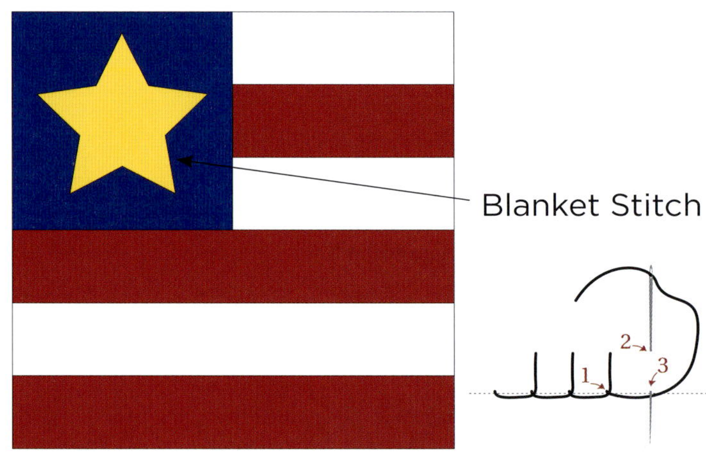

Optional: with two strands of embroidery floss, embroider the star with a blanket stitch.

 Shown in Quilter's Candy Basics by Connecting Threads.

6. Layer backing WS up, batting, and top WS down. Quilt. Bind with a ¼″ seam allowance. *Hint:* it is helpful to baste around the perimeter of the Itty Bitty Quilt ⅛″ before binding if quilting lightly.

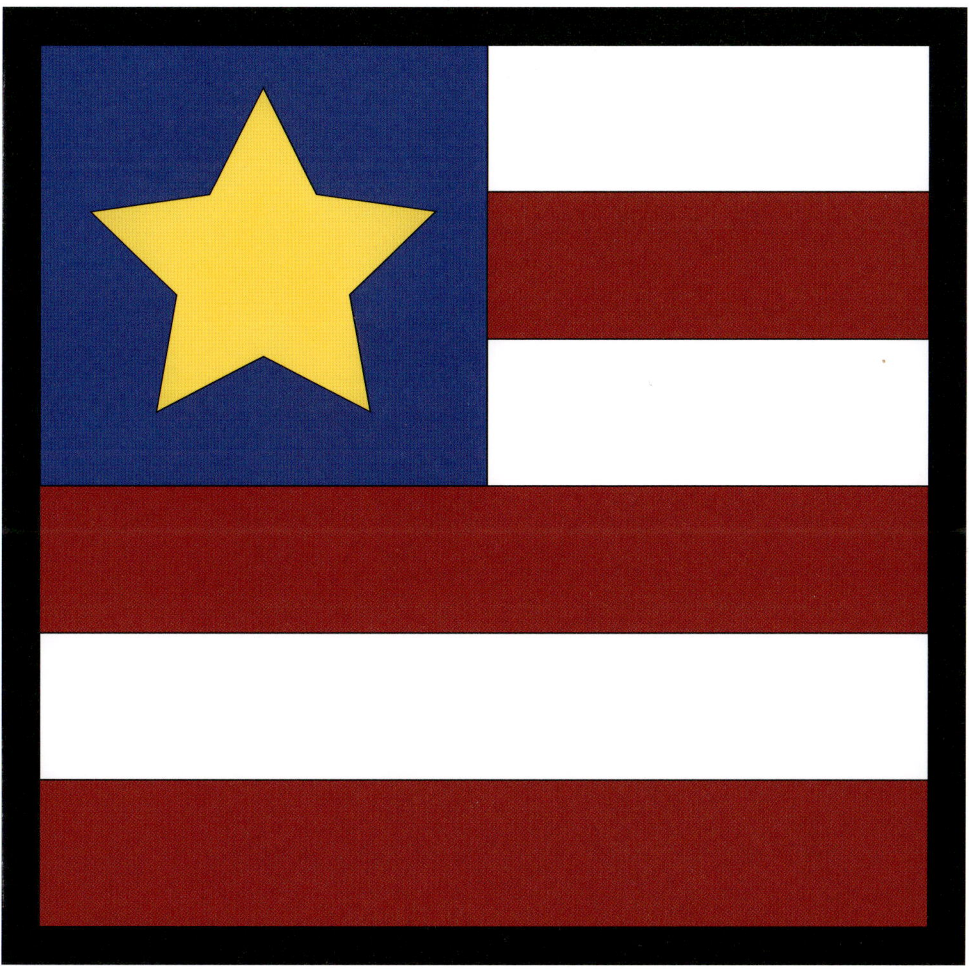

Itty Bitty August Leaf

Approx. finished size: 6½″ square

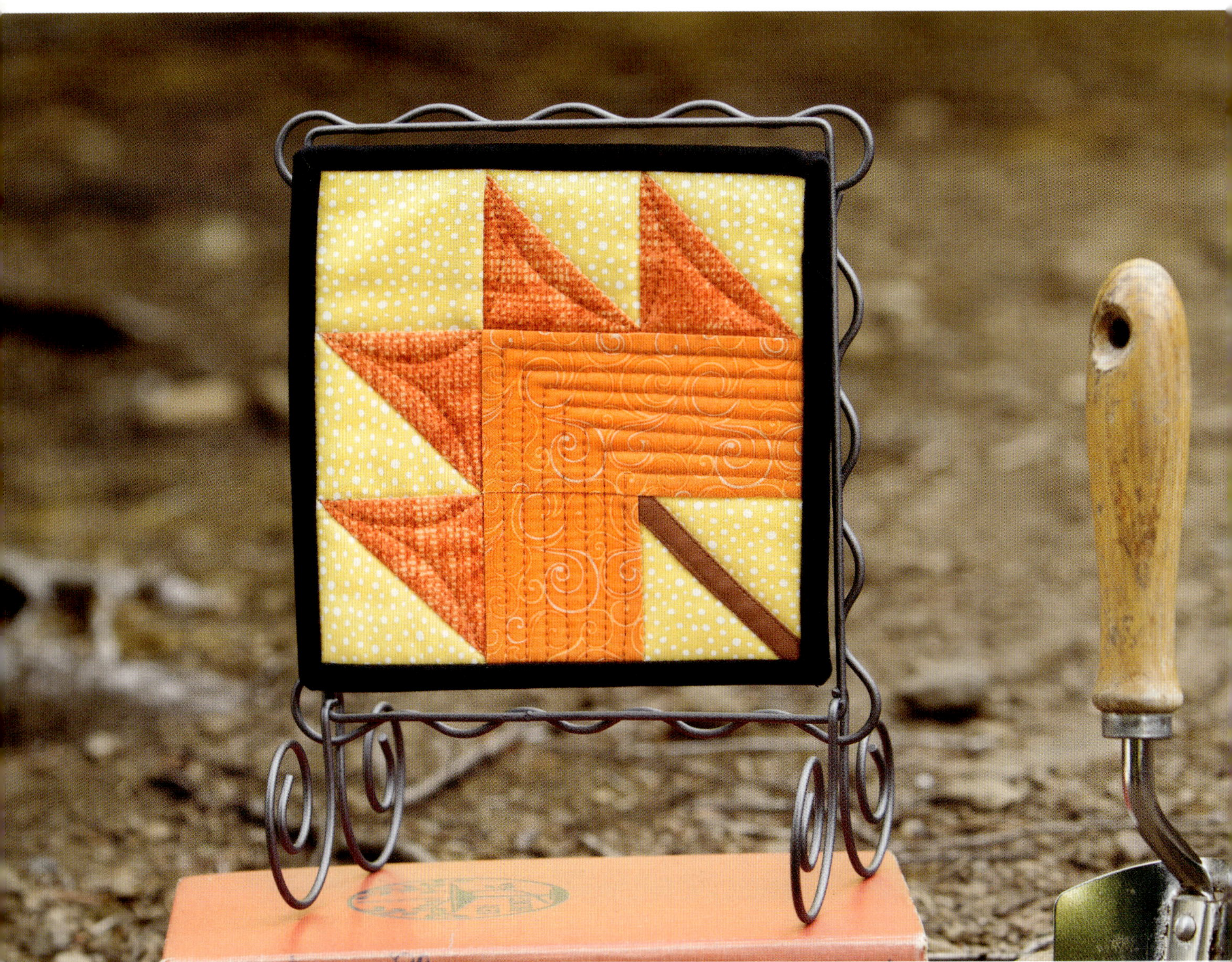

 Shown in Quilter's Candy Basics by Connecting Threads.

Connecting Threads Fabrics Used

- **Fabric 1:** Lotta Dots - Honeysuckle
- **Fabric 2:** Faux Burlap - Persimmon
- **Fabric 3:** Swirls - Orange
- **Fabric 4:** Solid - Curry

Please Note

Binding information for all Itty Bitty Quilts is on page 19.

Cutting suggestions are listed on pages 68 - 73.

Cutting Instructions

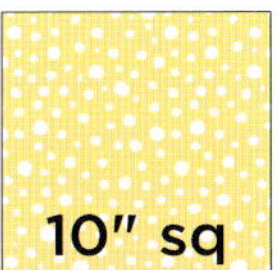

Fabric 1

A - Two 2⅞" squares

B - Two 2½" squares

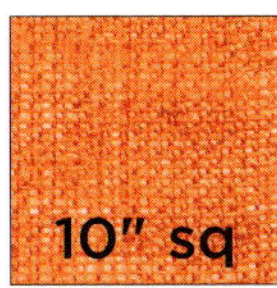

Fabric 2

C - Two 2⅞" squares

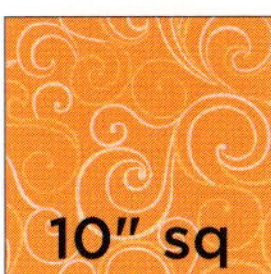

Fabric 3

D - One 2½" square

E - One 2½" x 4½"

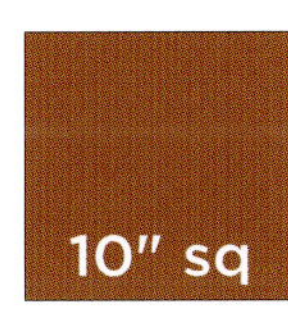

Fabric 4

F - One 1¼" x 3½"

Backing: An additional 9" square

Directions

1. Draw a diagonal line through all **A**s. Draw a line ¼″ on each side of the center diagonal line. Layer an **A** and a **C** together. Stitch slightly to the center of the ¼″ line and cut on the center line. Press.

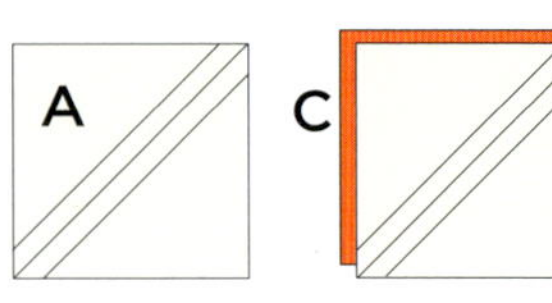

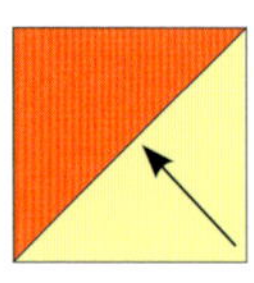

Make 4 ~ 2½″ square

2. Sew two **A/C** units together as shown. Press

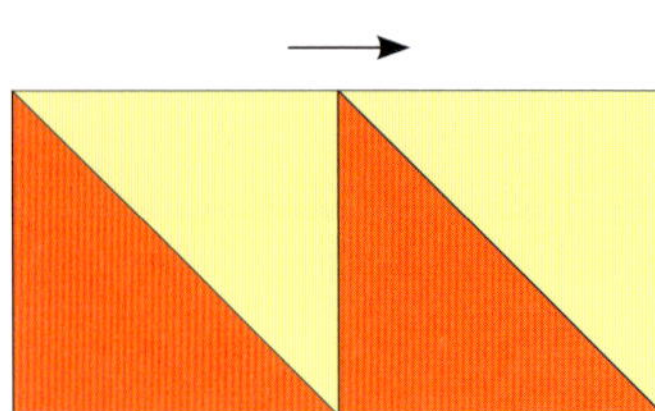

Make 1 ~ 2½″ x 4½″

3. Sew a **B** to the left side of the **A/C** unit from Step 2 as shown. Press.

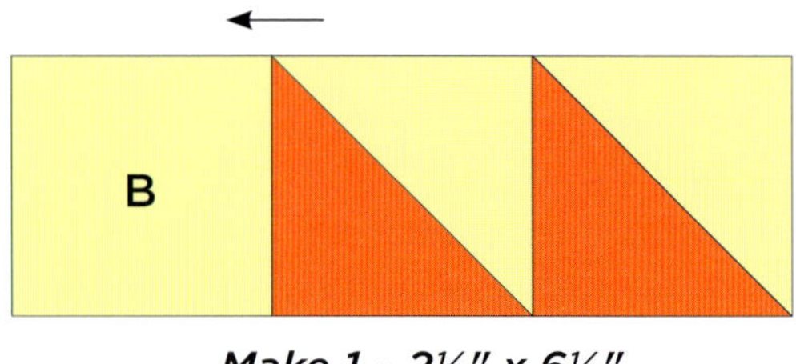

Make 1 ~ 2½″ x 6½″

4. Sew the remaining two units from Step 1 together as shown. Press.

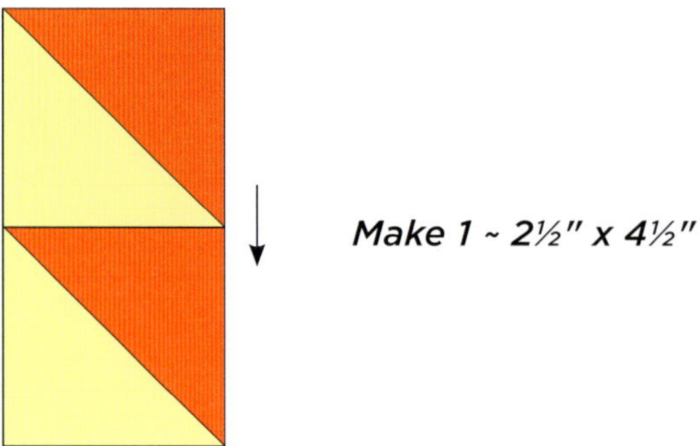

Make 1 ~ 2½″ x 4½″

5. Fold **F** in half along the long edge, WS together. Stitch ¼″. Trim seam to ⅛″. Open tube and flatten over the top of the seam hiding it. Press.

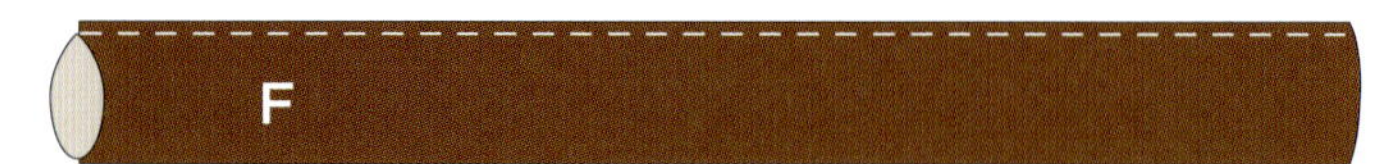

6. Lay **F** diagonally on a **B**, seam side down, and stitch ⅛″ along both folded edges. Press. Trim **F** to edges of **B** at the corners.

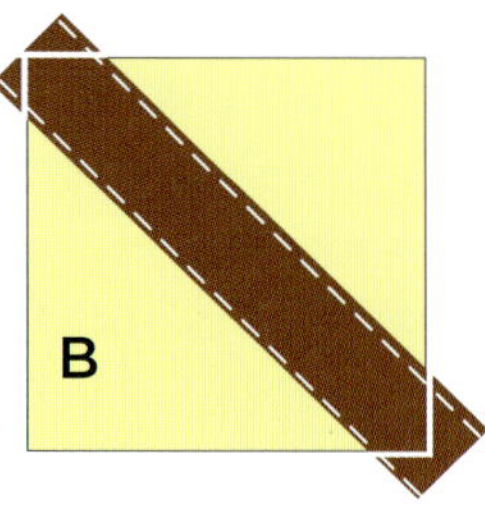

 Shown in Quilter's Candy Basics by Connecting Threads.

7. Sew a **D** to the Step 6 unit. Press. Sew the **D/B** unit to **E** as shown. Press.

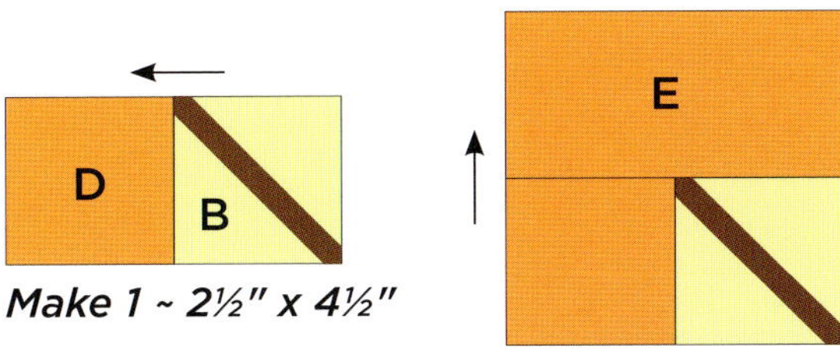

Make 1 ~ 2½" x 4½"

Make 1 ~ 4½" square

8. Sew the unit from Step 4 to the left side of the **D/B/E** unit. Press.

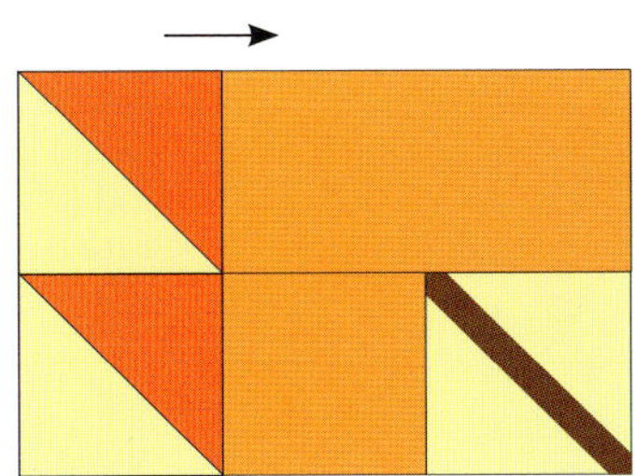

Make 1 ~ 4½" x 6½"

9. Sew the unit from Step 3 to the top of the unit from Step 8. Press.

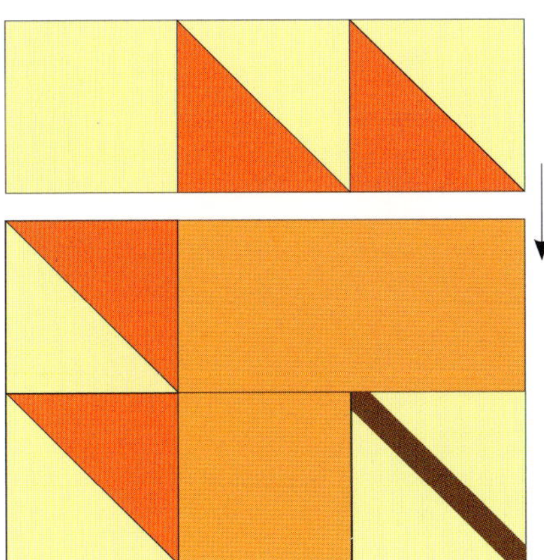

10. Layer backing WS up, batting, and top WS down. Quilt. Bind with a ¼" seam allowance. *Hint:* it is helpful to baste around the perimeter of the Itty Bitty Quilt ⅛" before binding if quilting lightly.

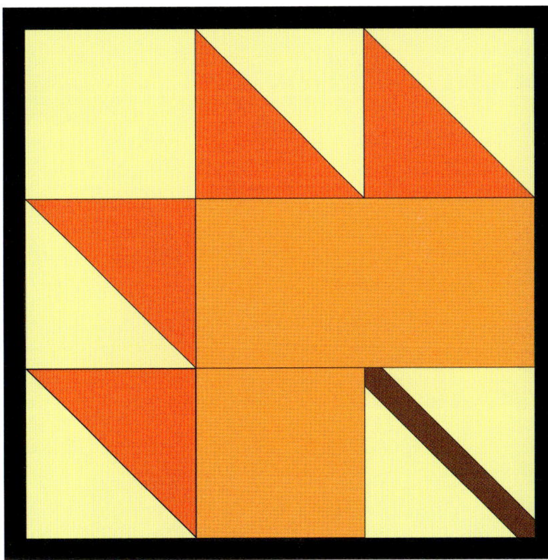

Itty Bitty September Apple

Approx. finished size: 6½″ square

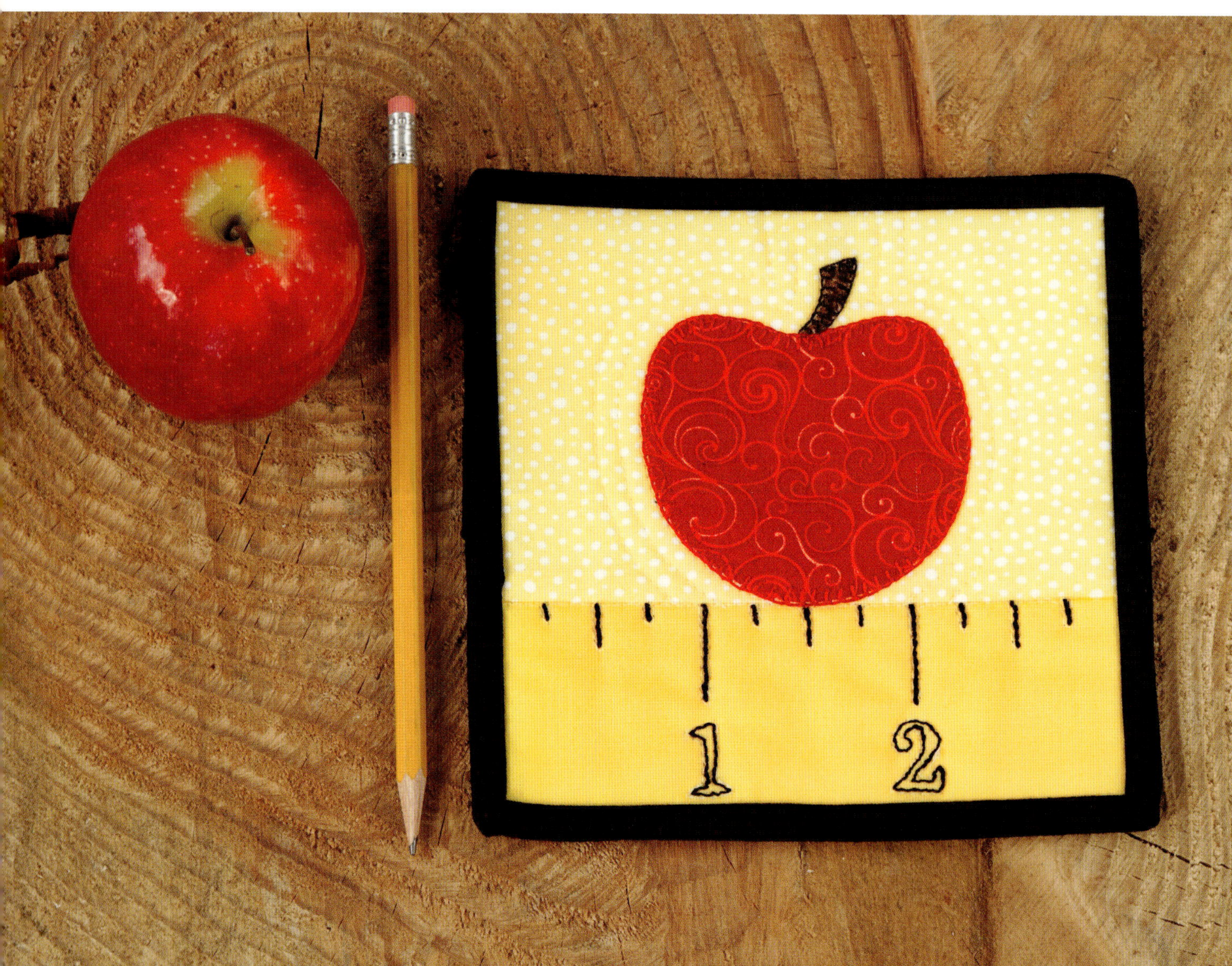

 Shown in Quilter's Candy Basics by Connecting Threads.

Connecting Threads Fabrics Used

- **Fabric 1:** Lotta Dots - Honeysuckle
- **Fabric 2:** Swirls - Red
- **Fabric 3:** Solid - Sun
- **Fabric 4:** Faux Burlap - Espresso

Additional Supplies

- 21294 Lite Steam-A-Seam 2®
- Black embroidery floss
- Brown and red embroidery floss (optional)
- Fusible woven interfacing (optional)

Please Note

Binding information for all Itty Bitty Quilts is on page 19.

Cutting suggestions are listed on pages 68 - 73.

Appliqué templates are listed on pages 74 - 78.

Cutting Instructions

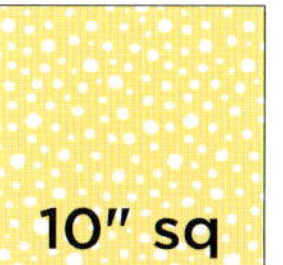

Fabric 1
A - One 4½″ x 6½″

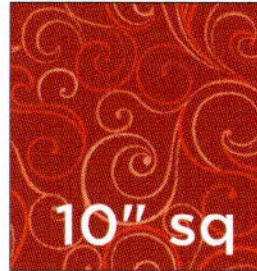

Fabric 2
B - One from template

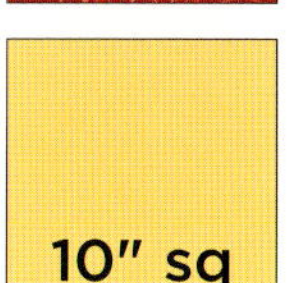

Fabric 3
C - One 2½″ x 6½″

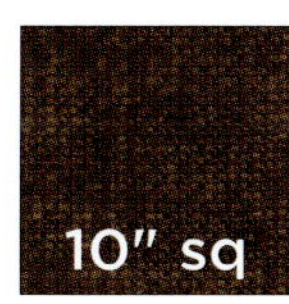

Fabric 4
D - One from template

Backing: An additional 9″ square

Directions

1. Sew **A** to **C**. Press.

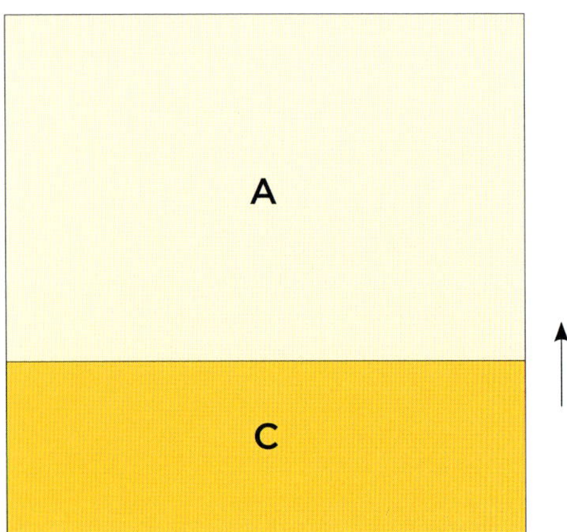

Embroidery

2. With two strands of black floss, embroider the lines on the ruler with a stem stitch and satin stitch the numbers. *Hint:* adhere fusible woven interfacing onto back to hide embroidery stitches.

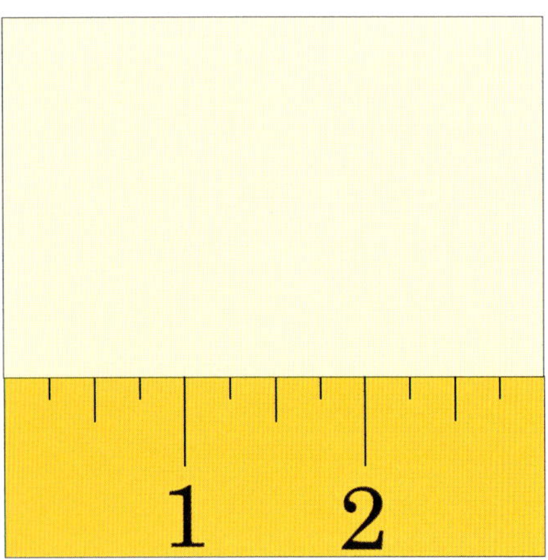

Satin Stitch

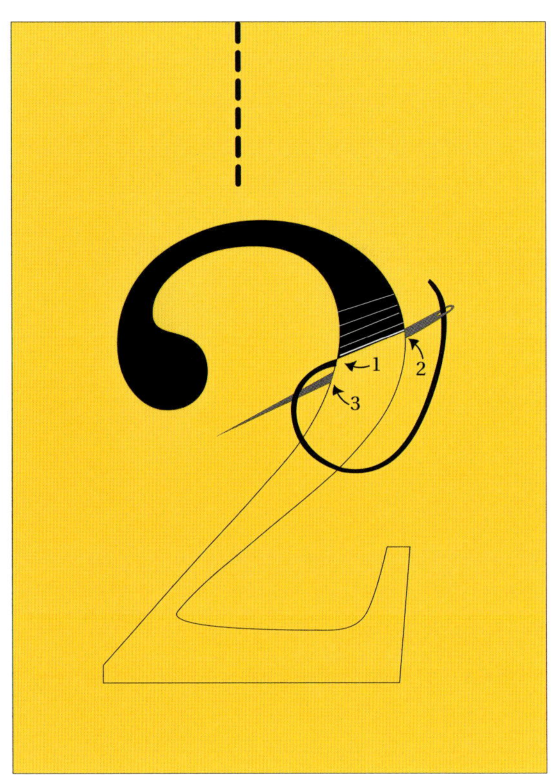

 Shown in Quilter's Candy Basics by Connecting Threads.

Appliqué

3. With appliqué method of choice, appliqué in the following order **D** and **B** to the little quilt.

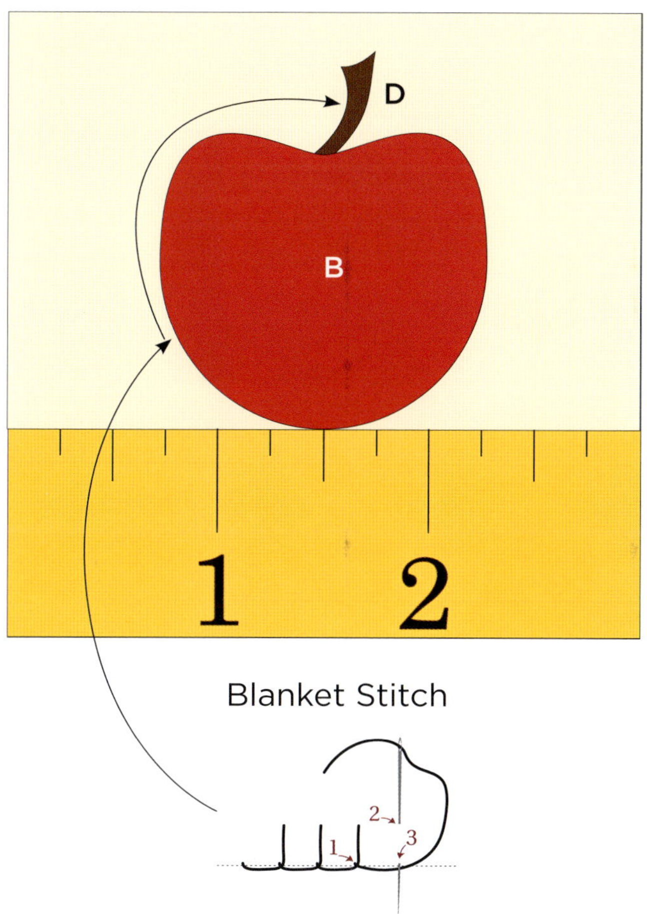

Optional: with two strands of embroidery floss, embroider the stem and apple with a blanket stitch.

4. Layer backing WS up, batting, and top WS down. Quilt. Bind with a ¼″ seam allowance. *Hint:* it is helpful to baste around the perimeter of the Itty Bitty Quilt ⅛″ before binding if quilting lightly.

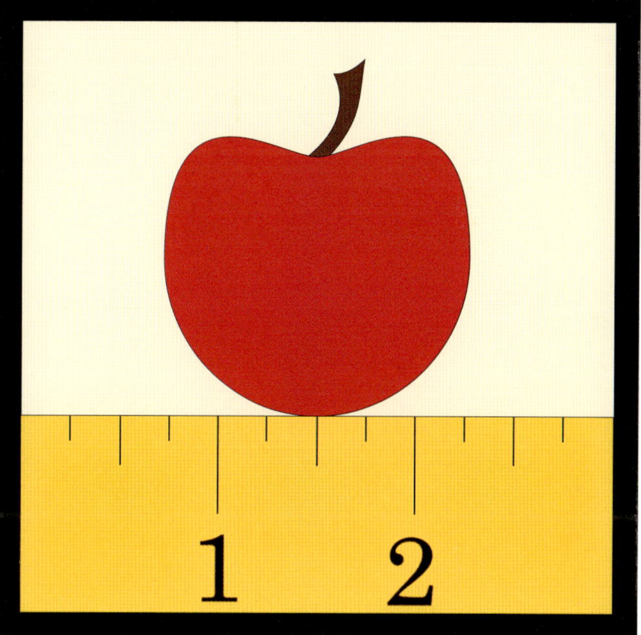

Itty Bitty October Mummy

Approx. finished size: 6½″ square

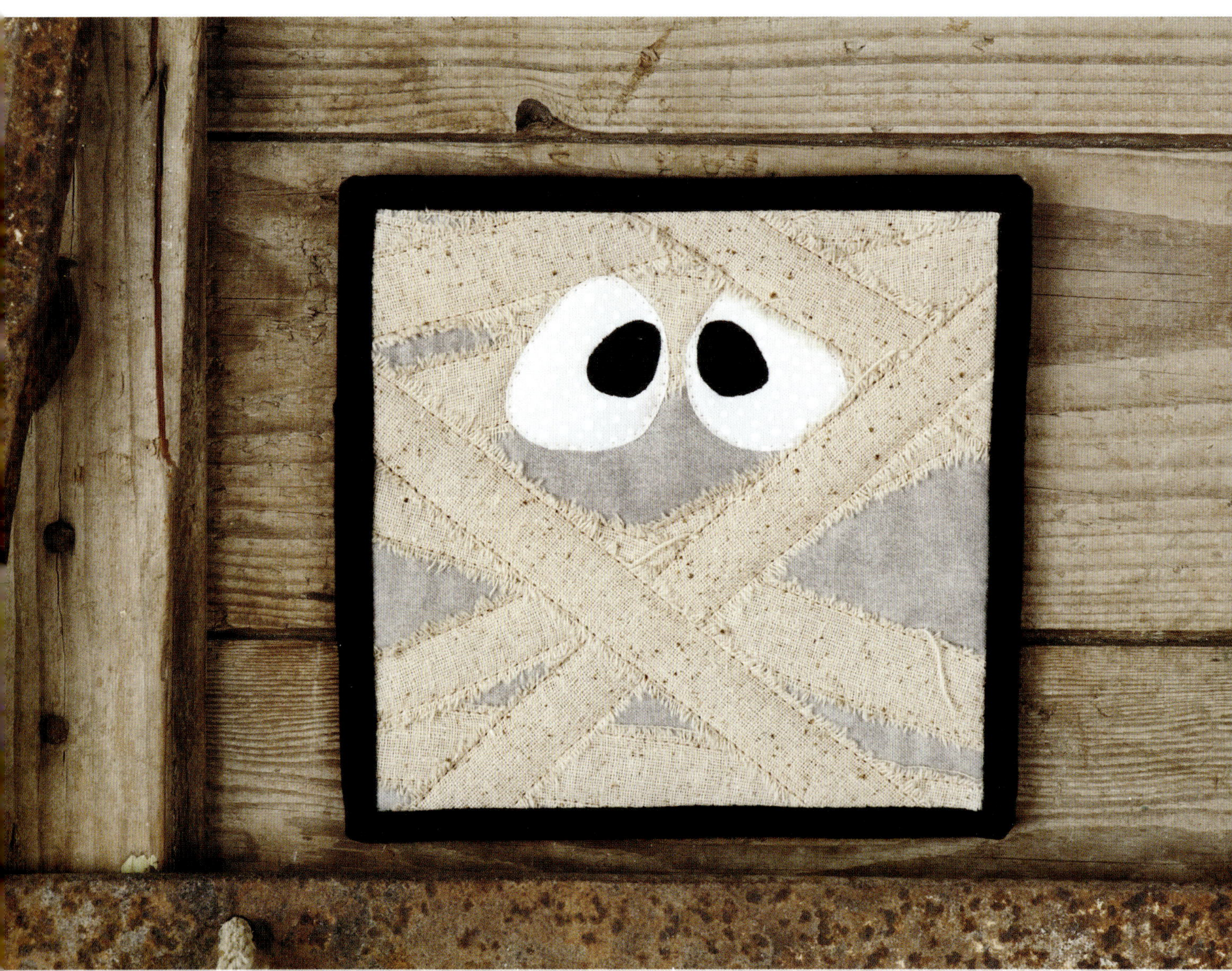

 Shown in Quilter's Candy Basics by Connecting Threads.

Connecting Threads Fabrics Used

- **Fabric 1:** Osnaburg – Natural
- **Fabric 2:** Solid – Black
- **Fabric 3:** Mirage – Silver Lining
- **Fabric 4:** Lotta Dots – White on White

Additional Supplies

- 21294 Lite Steam-A-Seam 2®

Helpful Tip

The construction of this Itty Bitty Quilt is designed using the quilt-as-you-go (QAYG) method. That is, as your are building the Itty Bitty Quilt, it is being quilted at the same time. When the construction of the quilt top is complete, so is the quilting!

Please Note

Binding information for all Itty Bitty Quilts is on page 19.

Cutting suggestions are listed on pages 68 – 73.

Appliqué templates are listed on pages 74 – 78.

Cutting Instructions

Fabric 1

A – Three 1″ x 18″
B – Three ¾″ x 18″

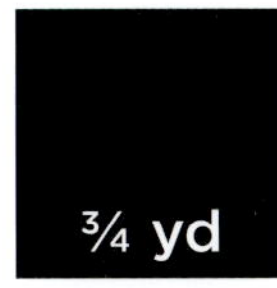

Fabric 2

E – Two from template

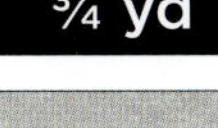

Fabric 3

C – One 7″ square

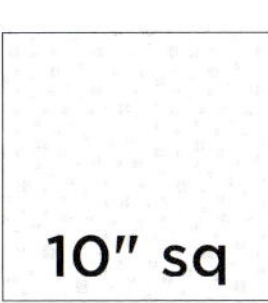

Fabric 4

D – Two from template

Backing: An additional 9″ square

Directions

1. Cut or tear (preferable) three **A**s and three **B**s from the fat quarter. Layer backing WS up, batting, and **C**, WS down. Top stitch **A**s and **B**s onto **C**. Trim tail off. *Hint:* the torn fabric will fray the edges, thus making the bandages look more realistic. Also, the strips can be irregular in width.

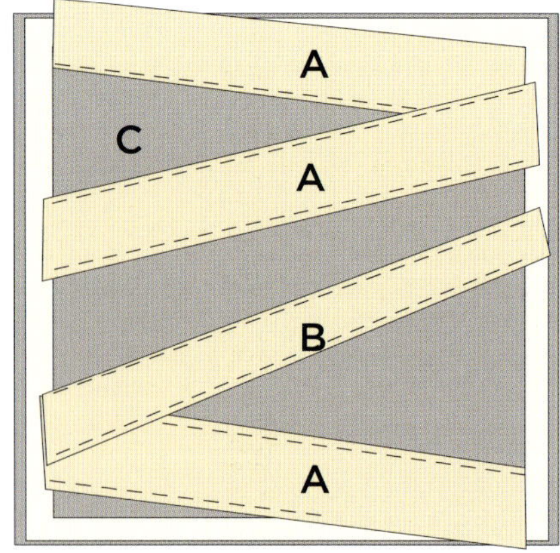

2. Add another layer of **B**s randomly top stitching them to **C**. *Hint:* the previous **A**s and **B**s were lightened to more easily see the placement for new strips.

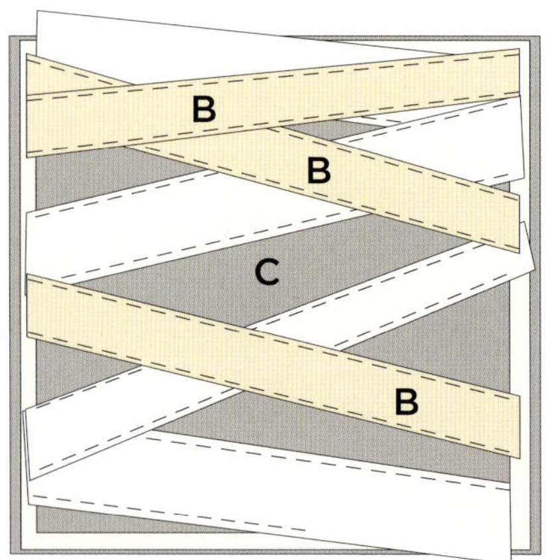

Appliqué

3. Using appliqué method of choice, center and appliqué **D**s and **E**s to the little quilt unit.

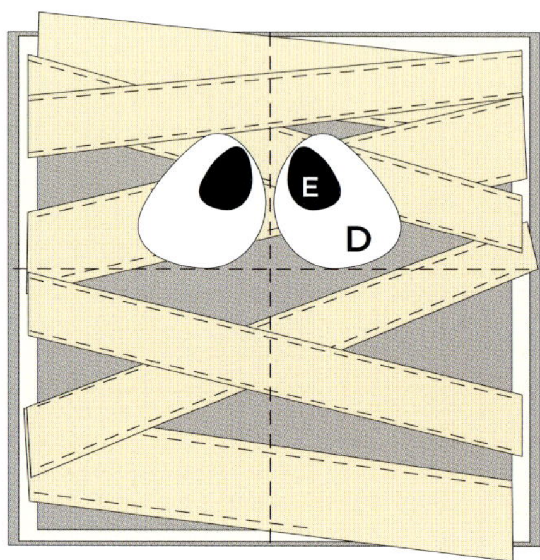

4. Add the final layer of **A**s to **C**, slightly covering up the eyes. Trim to 6½" square.

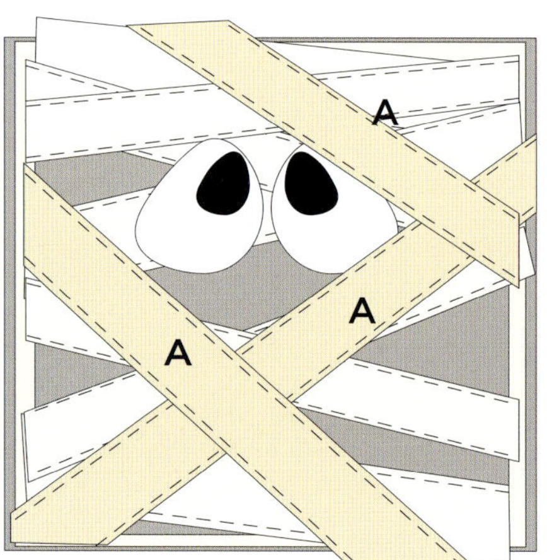

 Shown in Quilter's Candy Basics by Connecting Threads.

5. Bind with a ¼″ seam allowance.

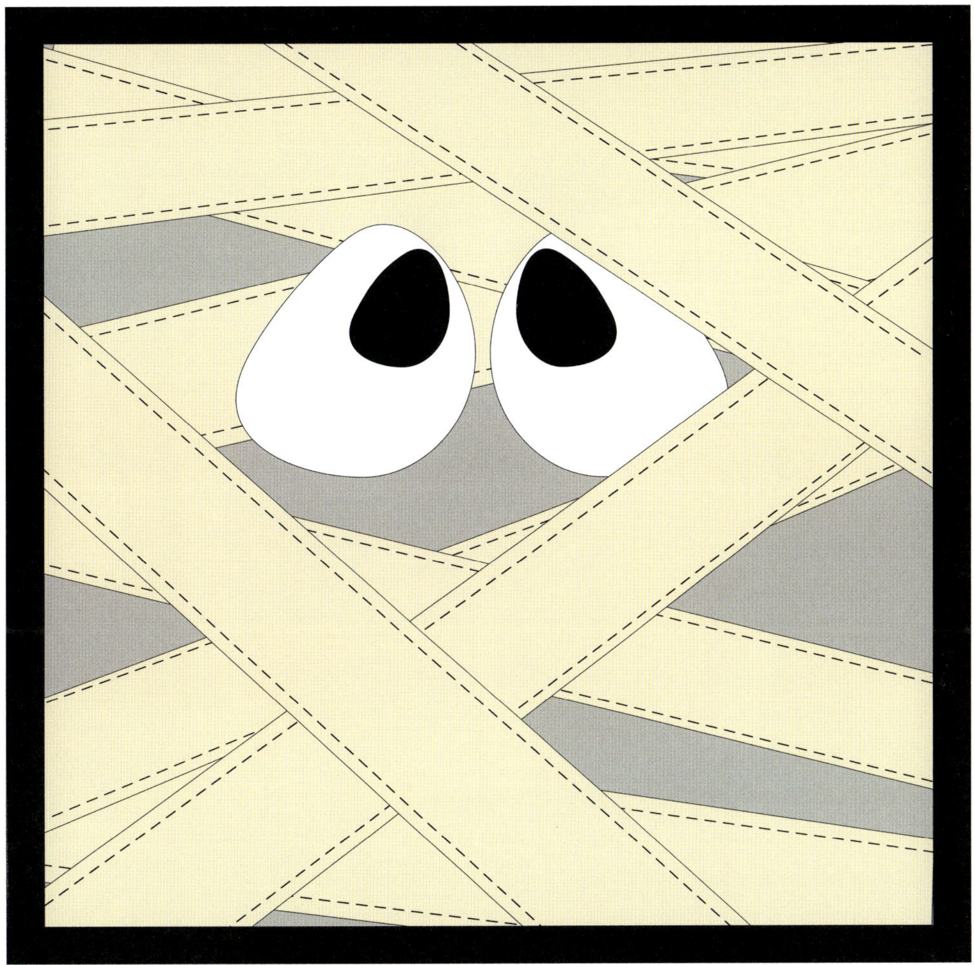

Itty Bitty November Pumpkin

Approx. finished size: 6½″ square

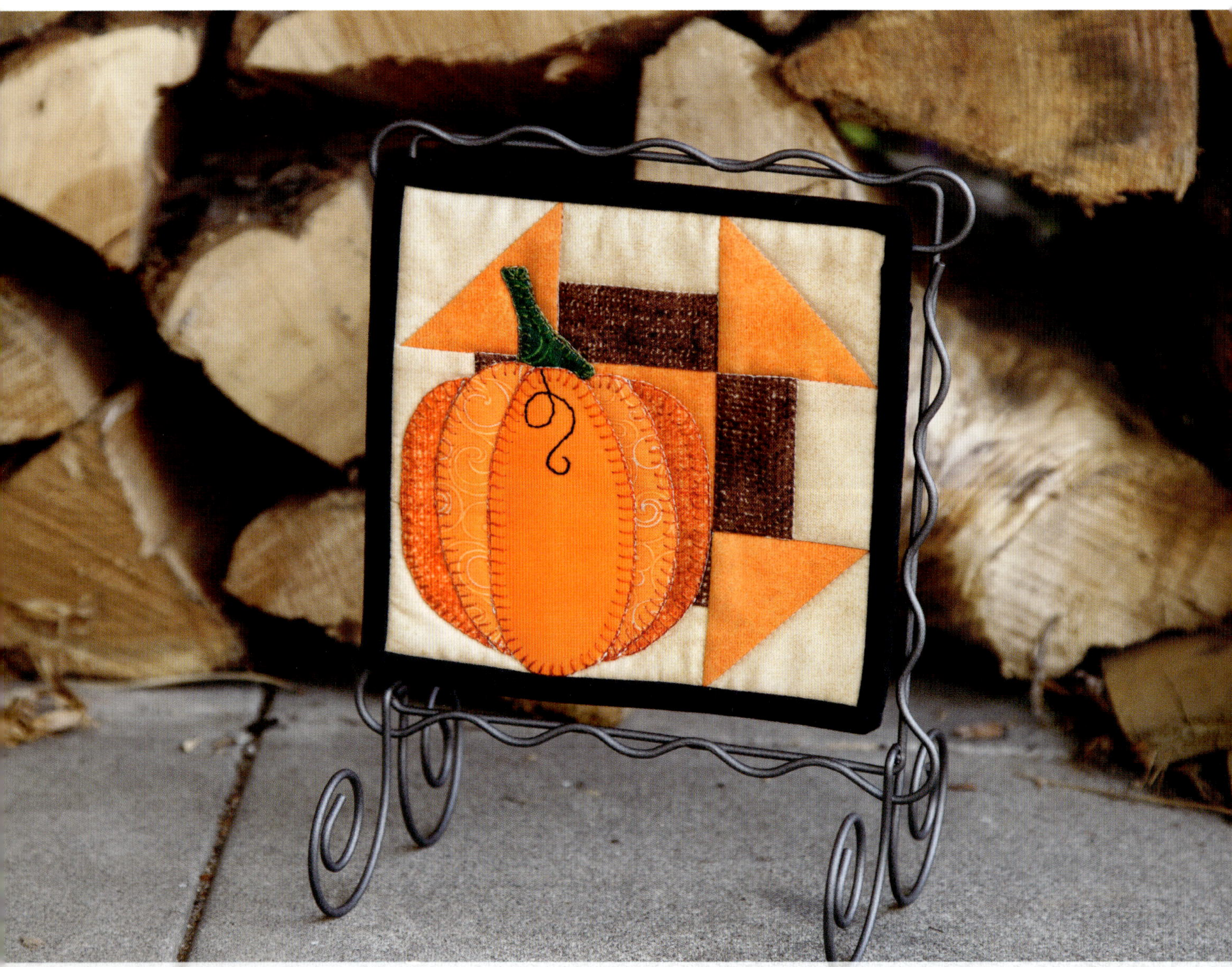

 Shown in Quilter's Candy Basics by Connecting Threads.

Connecting Threads Fabrics Used

- **Fabric 1:** Mirage - Antique
- **Fabric 2:** Mirage - Orange
- **Fabric 3:** Faux Burlap - Espresso
- **Fabric 4:** Faux Burlap - Persimmon
- **Fabric 5:** Swirls - Orange
- **Fabric 6:** Solid - Orangina
- **Fabric 7:** Swirls - Ivy

Additional Supplies

- 21294 Lite Steam-A-Seam 2®
- Black embroidery floss
- Dark orange, medium orange, light orange, and green embroidery floss (optional)
- Fusible woven interfacing (optional)

Please Note

Binding information for all Itty Bitty Quilts is on page 19.

Cutting suggestions are listed on pages 68 - 73.

Appliqué templates are listed on pages 74 - 78.

Cutting Instructions

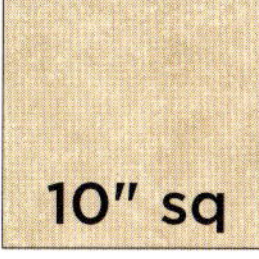

Fabric 1

A - Two 2⅞″ squares

B - Four 1½″ x 2½″

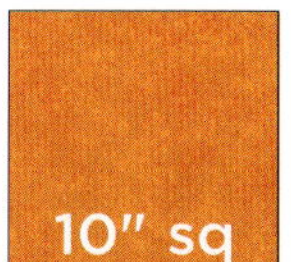

Fabric 2

C - Two 2⅞″ squares

D - One 2½″ square

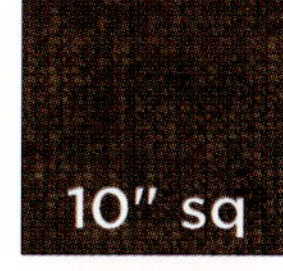

Fabric 3

E - Four 1½″ x 2½″

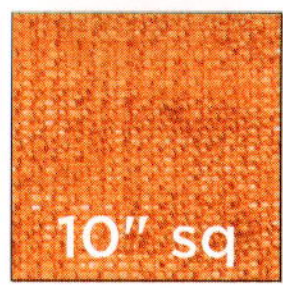

Fabric 4

F - One from template

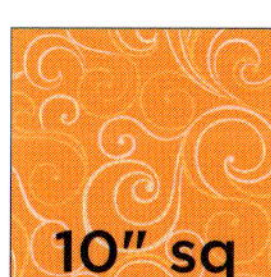

Fabric 5

G - One from template

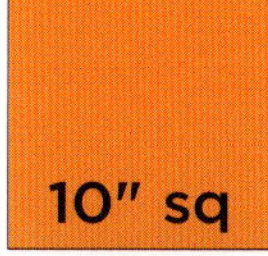

Fabric 6

H - One from template

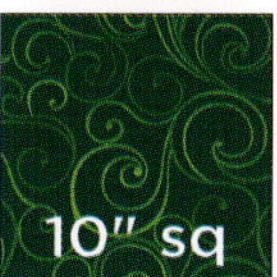

Fabric 7

J - One from template

Backing: An additional 9″ square

Directions

1. Draw a diagonal line through all **A**s. Draw a line ¼" on each side of the center diagonal line. Layer an **A** and a **C** together. Stitch slightly to the center of the ¼" line and cut on the center line. Press.

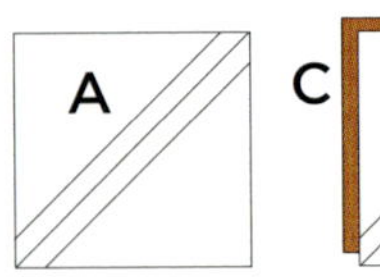

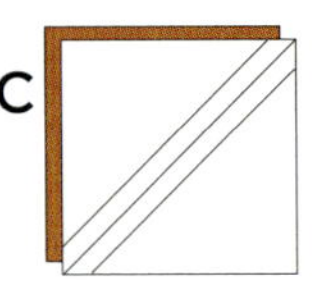

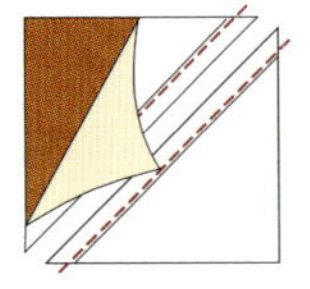
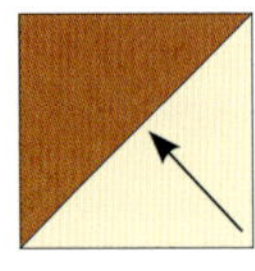

Make 4 ~ 2½" square

2. Sew a **B** and **E** together as shown. Press.

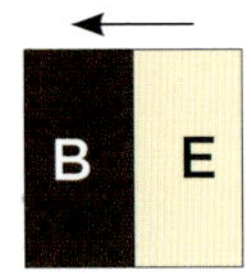

Make 4 ~ 2½" square

3. Sew an **A/C** unit to facing sides of a **B/E** unit oriented as shown. Press.

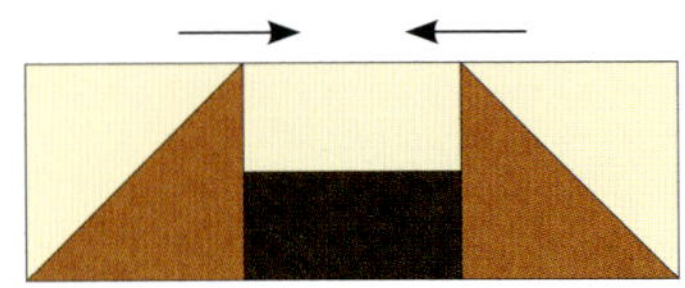

Make 2 ~ 2½" x 6½"

4. Sew a **B/E** unit to facing sides of a **D** oriented as shown. Press.

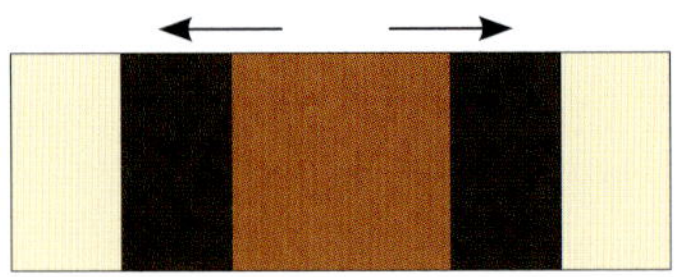

Make 1 ~ 2½" x 6½"

5. Sew a unit from Step 3 to facing sides of the unit from Step 4. Press.

 Shown in Quilter's Candy Basics by Connecting Threads.

6. Using preferred method of appliqué, appliqué in the following order, **J**, **F**, **G**, and **H** to the little quilt being aware of the ¼″ seam allowance. With two strands of floss, embroider the tendril to the pumpkin with a back stitch.

7. Layer backing WS up, batting, and top WS down. Quilt. Bind with a ¼″ seam allowance. *Hint:* it is helpful to baste around the perimeter of the Itty Bitty Quilt ⅛″ before binding if quilting lightly.

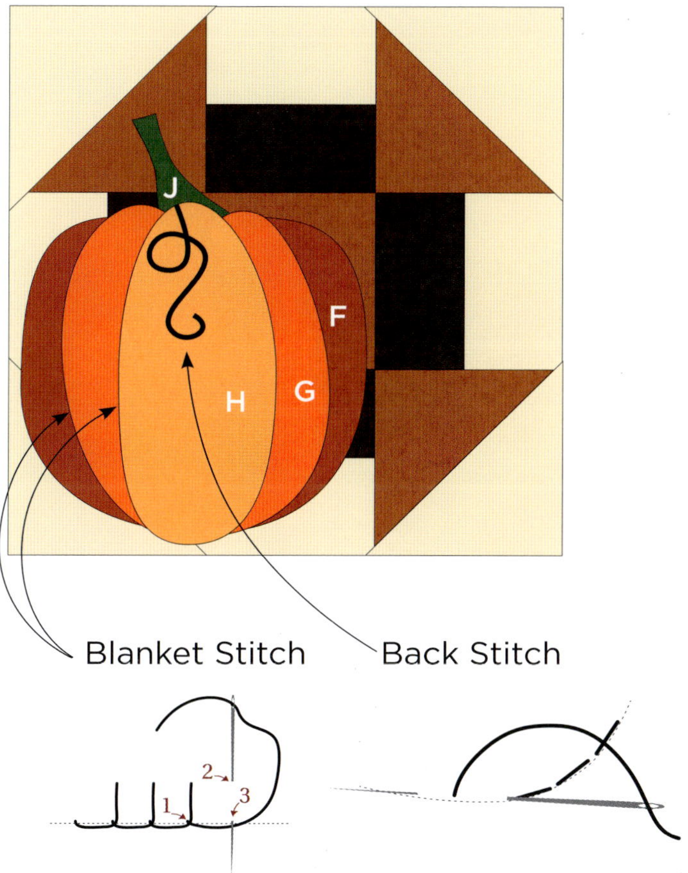

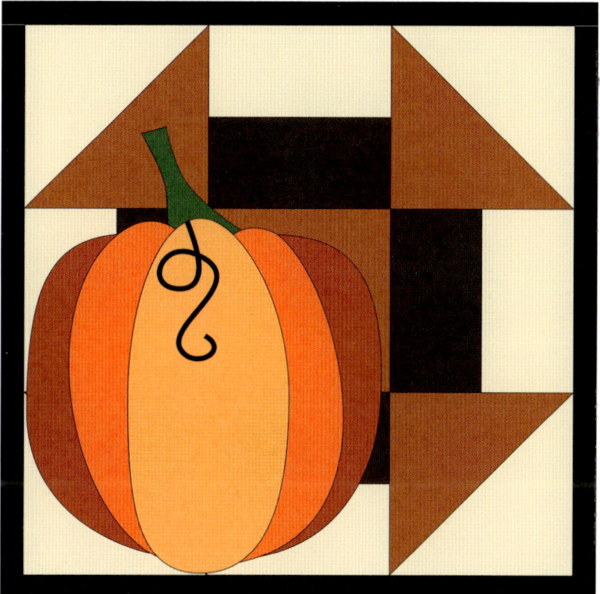

Optional: with two strands of embroidery floss, embroider the pumpkin sections and stem with a blanket stitch.

Itty Bitty December Candy Canes

Approx. finished size: 6½″ square

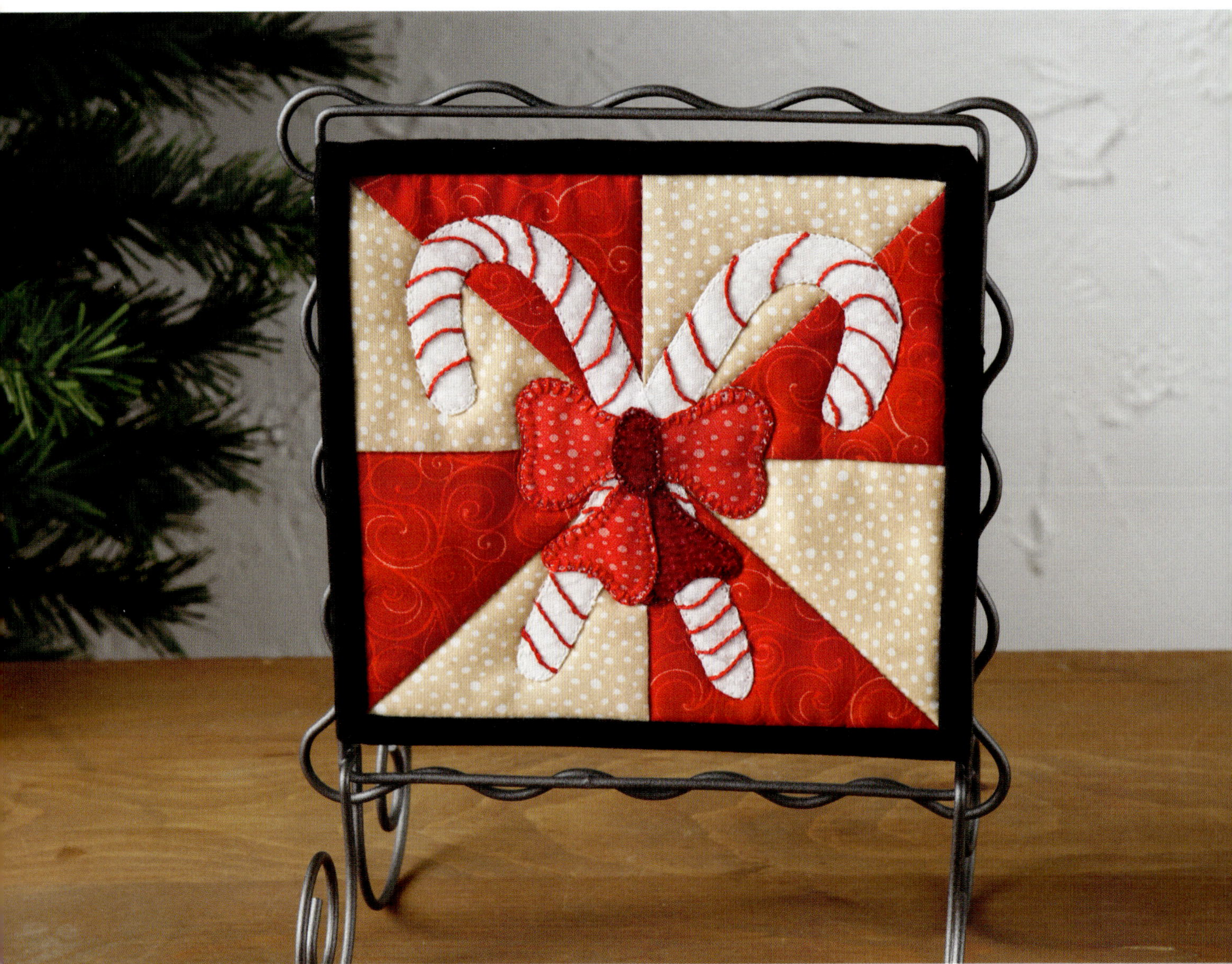

 Shown in Quilter's Candy Basics by Connecting Threads.

Connecting Threads Fabrics Used

- **Fabric 1:** Lotta Dots - Antique
- **Fabric 2:** Swirls - Red
- **Fabric 3:** Lotta Dots - White on White
- **Fabric 4:** Lotta Dots - Tomato
- **Fabric 5:** Faux Burlap - Merlot

Additional Supplies

- 21294 Lite Steam-A-Seam 2®
- Red embroidery floss
- Fusible woven interfacing (optional)

Please Note

Binding information for all Itty Bitty Quilts is on page 19.

Cutting suggestions are listed on pages 68 - 73.

Appliqué templates are listed on pages 74 - 78.

Cutting Instructions

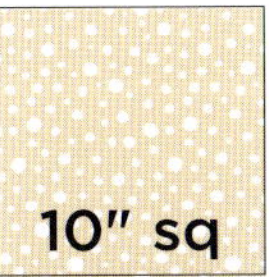

Fabric 1
A - Two 3⅞" squares

Fabric 2
B - Two 3⅞" squares

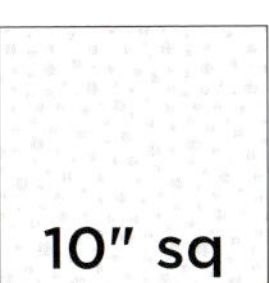

Fabric 3
C - Two from template

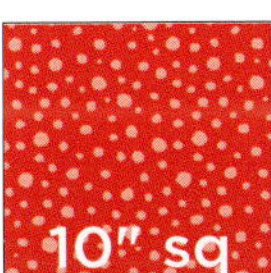

Fabric 4
D - One from template
G - One from template

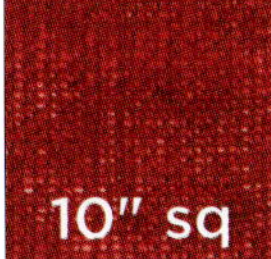

Fabric 5
E - One from template
F - One from template

Backing: An additional 9" square

Directions

1. Draw a diagonal line through all **A**s. Draw a line ¼″ on each side of the center diagonal line. Layer an **A** and a **B** together. Stitch slightly to the center of the ¼″ line and cut on the center line. Press.

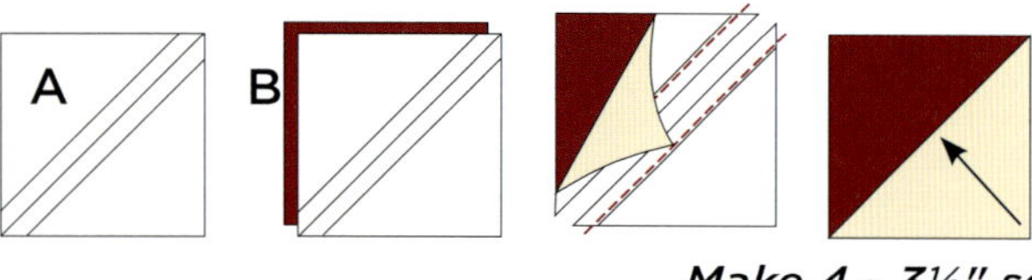

Make 4 ~ 3½″ sq

2. Sew two **A/B** units together as shown. Press. Repeat.

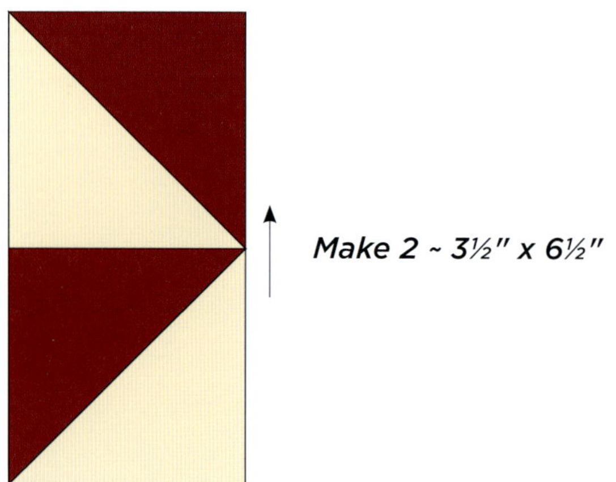

Make 2 ~ 3½″ x 6½″

3. Sew the two **A/B** unit together turning one unit 180°. Press.

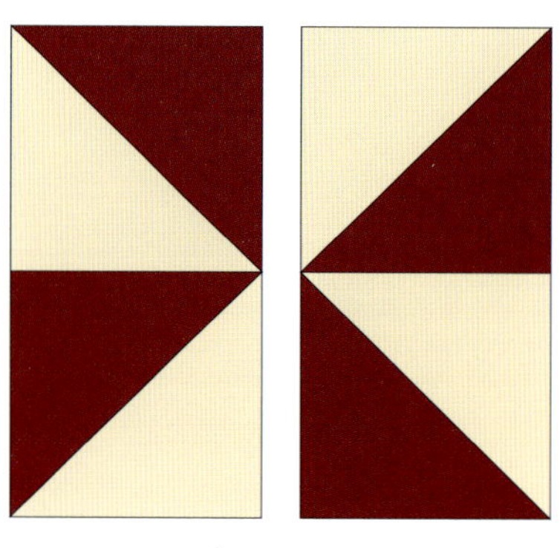

Appliqué/Embroidery

4. Using appliqué method of choice, appliqué the **C**s to the quilt. Embroider stripes on **C**s with a back stitch. *Hint:* adhere fusible woven interfacing onto back to hide embroidery stitches.

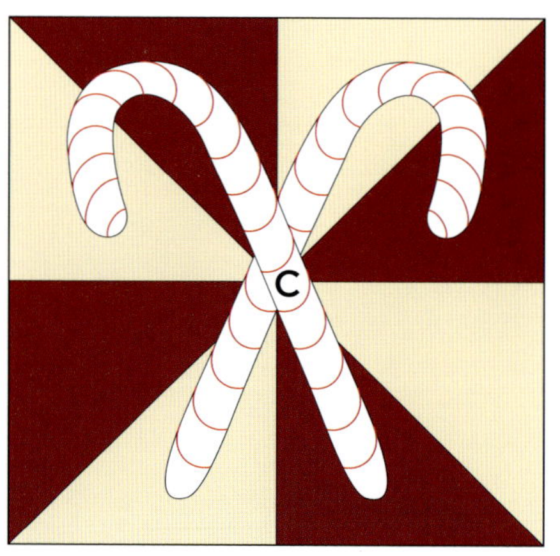

 Shown in Quilter's Candy Basics by Connecting Threads.

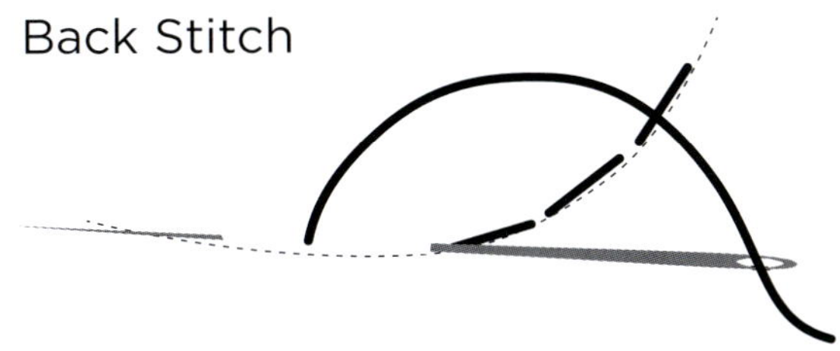

5. Appliqué in the following order, **D**, **E**, **G**, and **F** to the quilt.

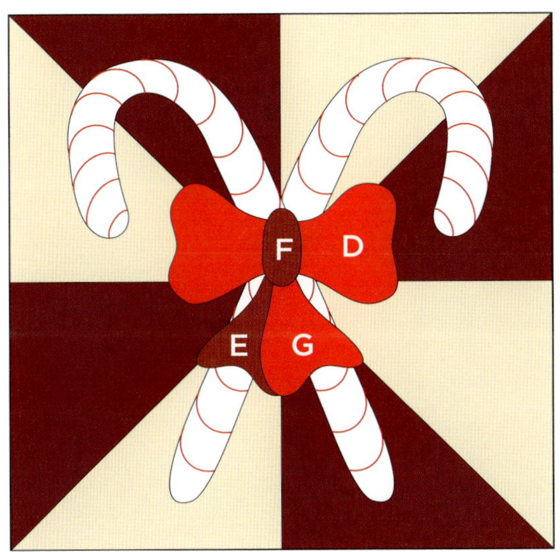

6. Layer backing WS up, batting, and top WS down. Quilt. Bind with a ¼″ seam allowance. *Hint:* it is helpful to baste around the perimeter of the Itty Bitty Quilt ⅛″ before binding if quilting lightly.

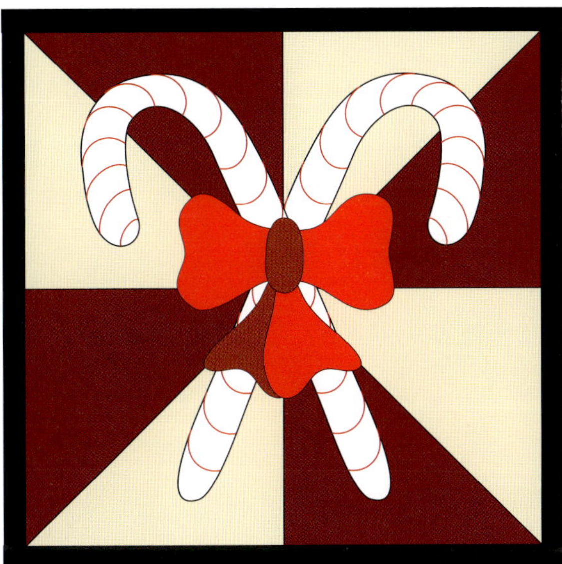

Cutting Suggestions For *All Itty Bitty Quilts*

Each pattern's cutting requirements are listed on the first page of each pattern within this book.

These pages are meant to be used as a cutting suggestions guide if you plan on making all of the Itty Bitty Quilts using the 10" Stack (#8666 on our website **ConnectingThreads.com**). Because many of the fabrics are used in multiple Itty Bitty Quilts, we have named each piece or template with the patterns they match—such as "Sept. A" which means it coordinates with the Itty Bitty Quilt - September, and fabric cut "A".

10" Squares

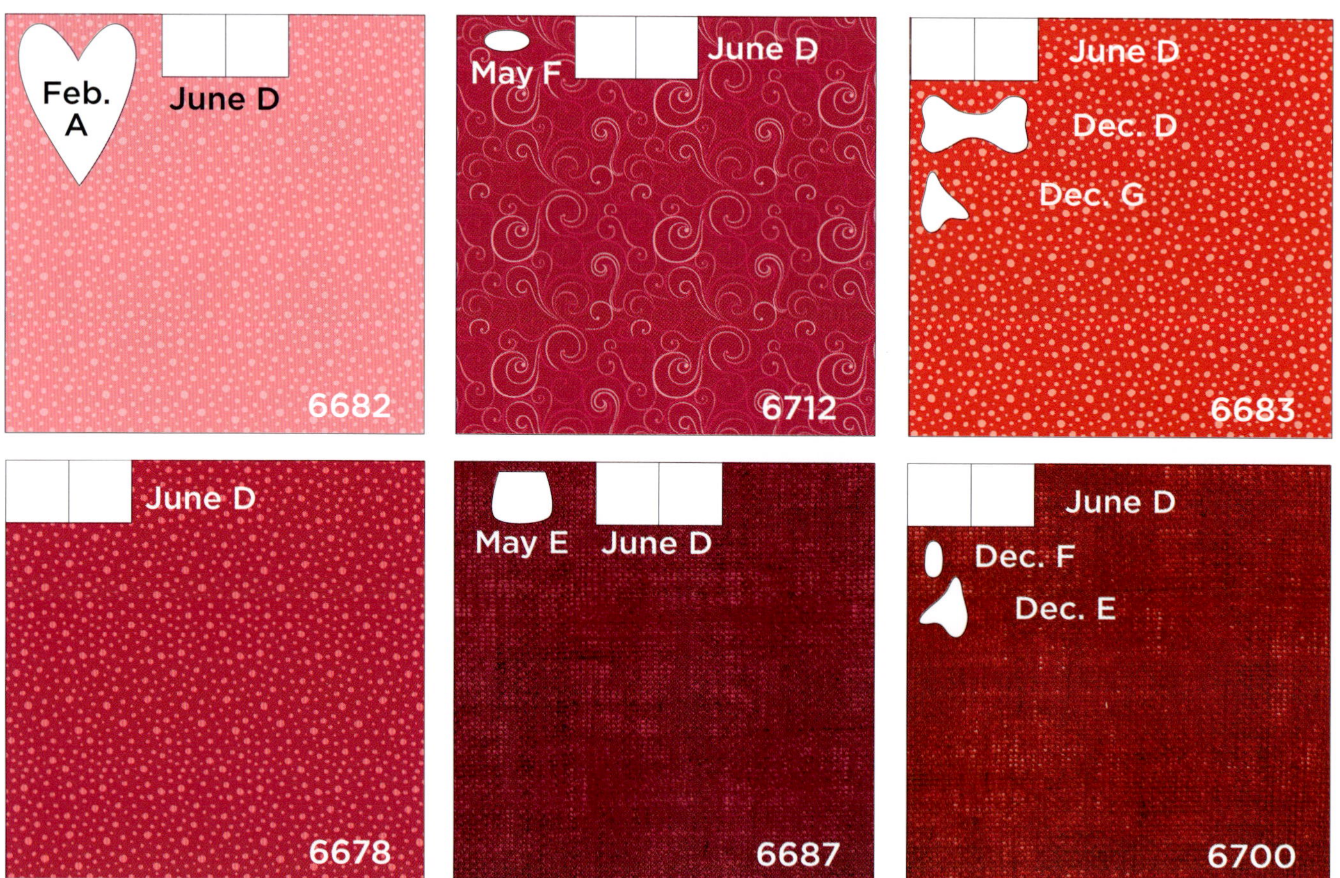

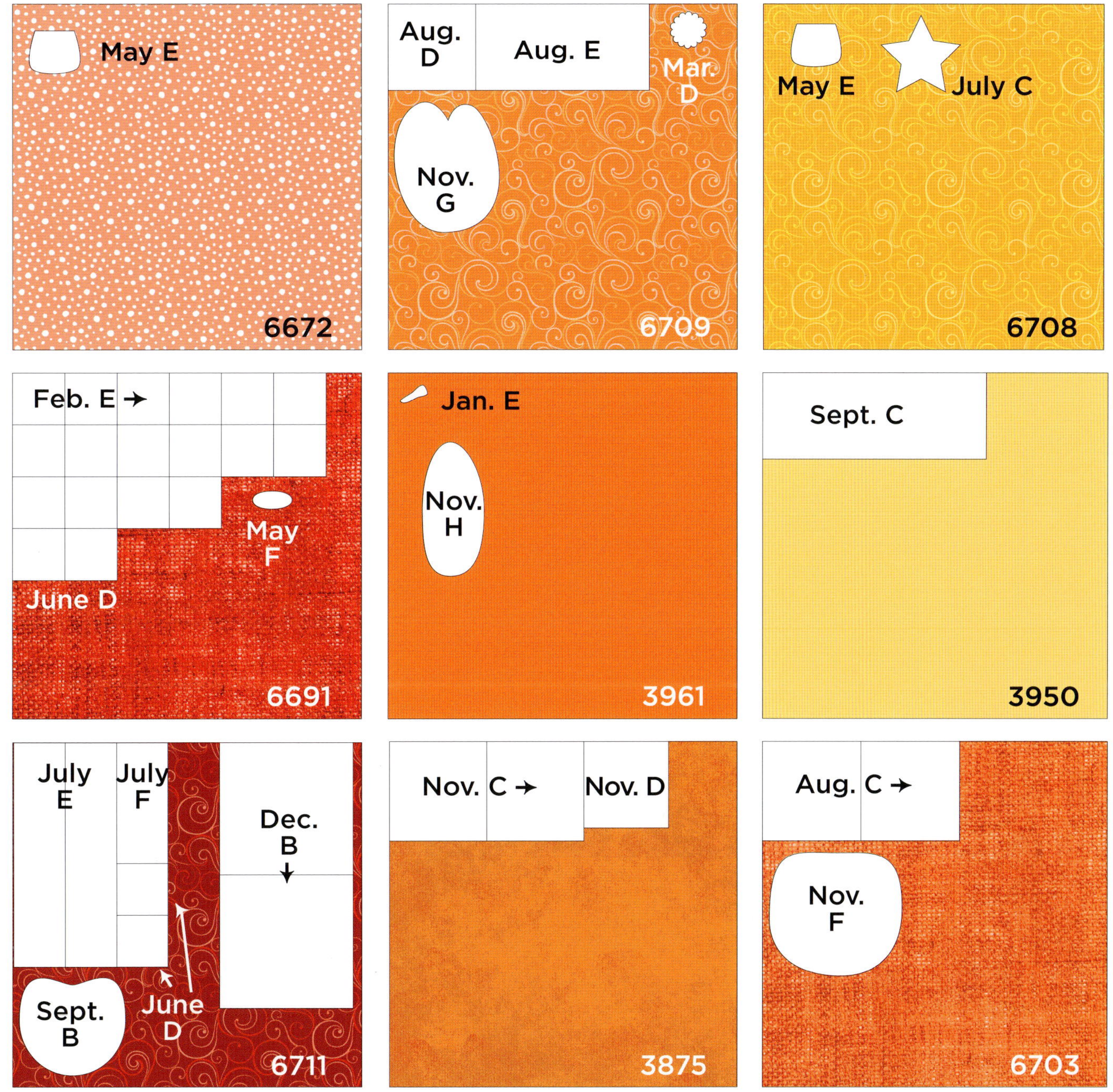
May E
6672
Aug. D
Aug. E
Mar. D
Nov. G
6709
May E
July C
6708
Feb. E →
May F
June D
6691
Jan. E
Nov. H
3961
Sept. C
3950
July E
July F
Dec. B
Sept. B
June D
6711
Nov. C →
Nov. D
3875
Aug. C →
Nov. F
6703

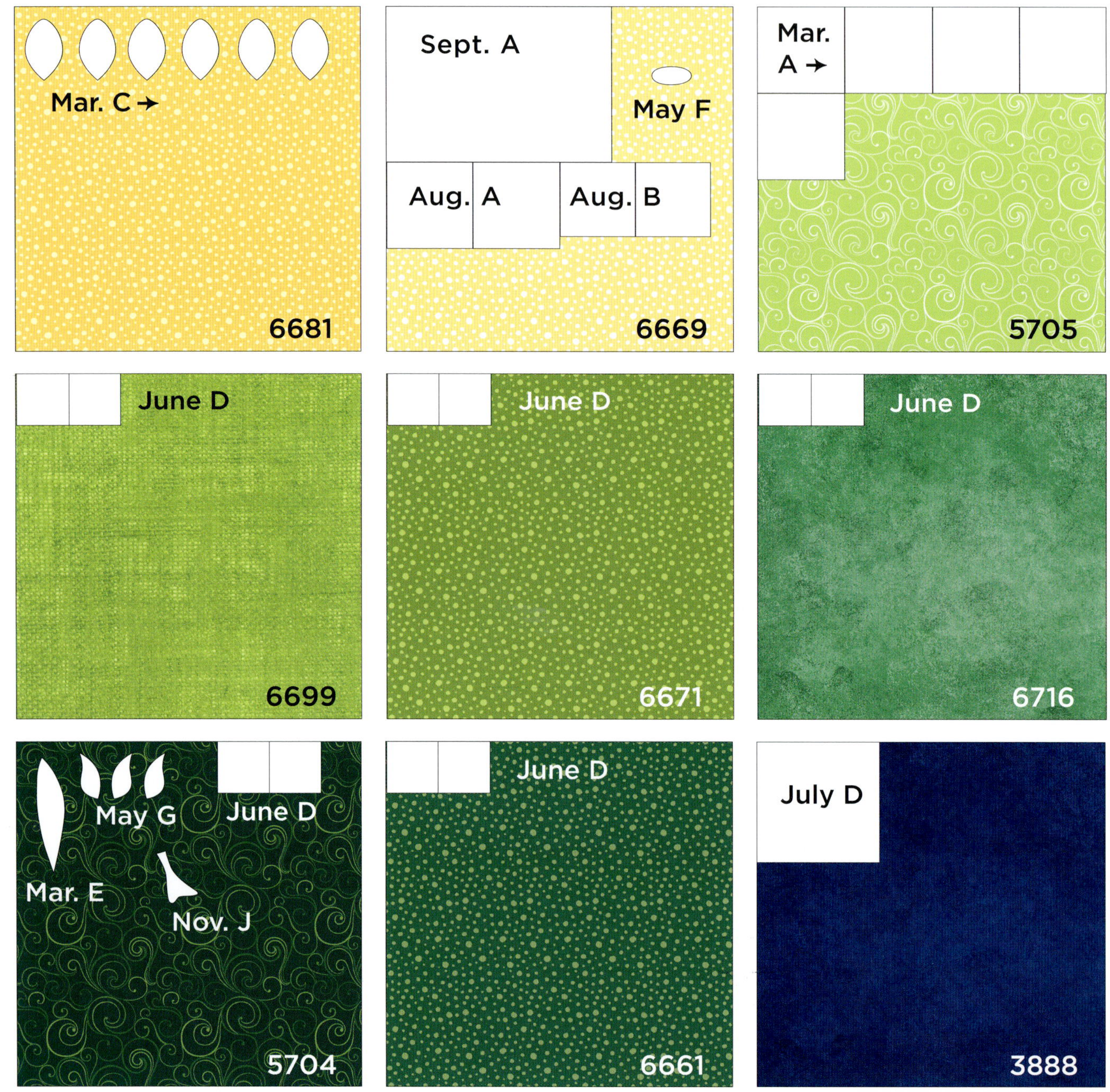

Mar. C →
6681
Sept. A
May F
Aug. A
Aug. B
6669
Mar.
A →
5705
June D
6699
June D
6671
June D
6716
May G
June D
Mar. E
Nov. J
5704
June D
6661
July D
3888

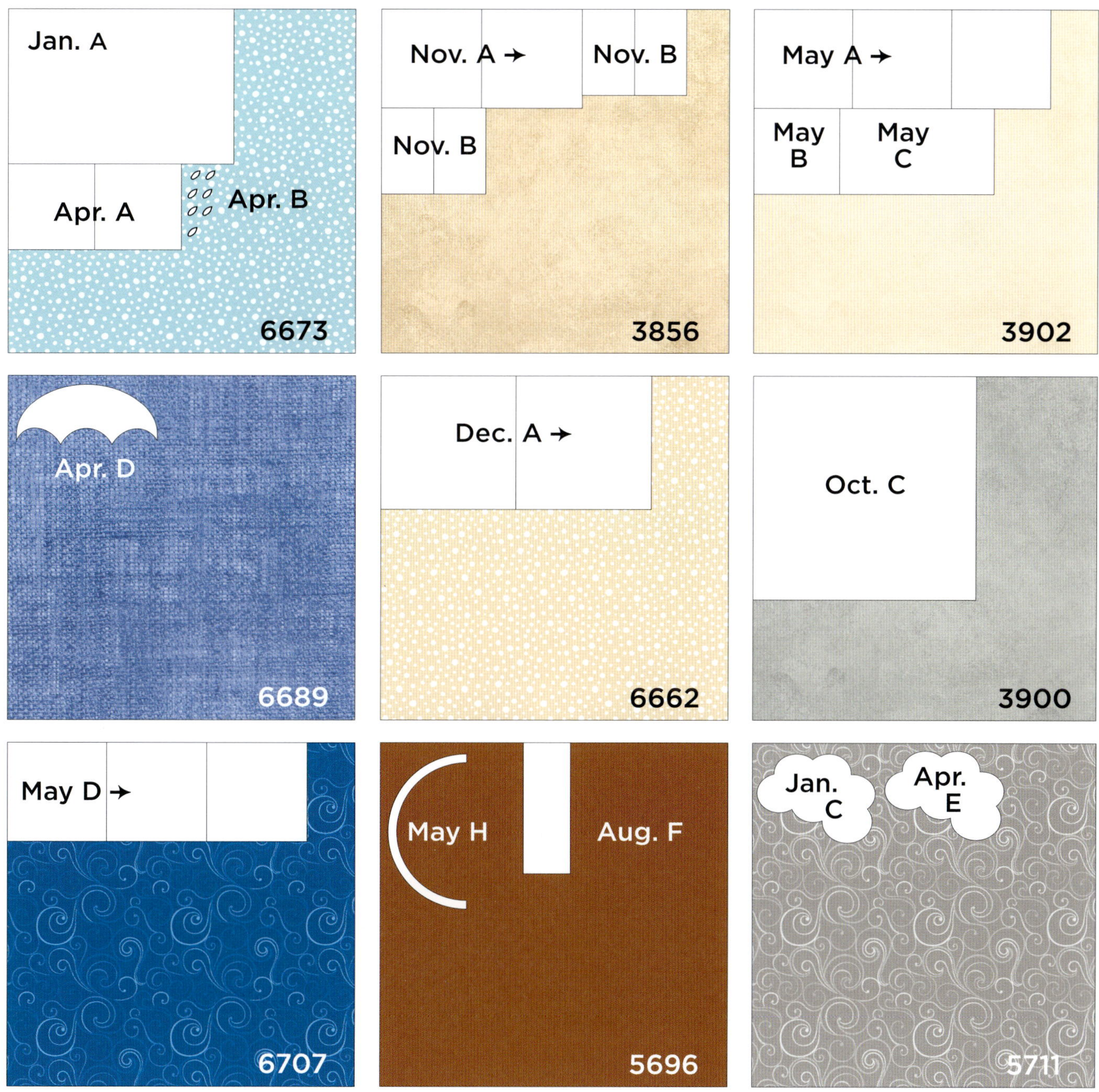
Jan. A
Apr. A
Apr. B
6673
Nov. A →
Nov. B
Nov. B
3856
May A →
May B
May C
3902
Apr. D
6689
Dec. A →
6662
Oct. C
3900
May D →
6707
May H
Aug. F
5696
Jan. C
Apr. E
5711

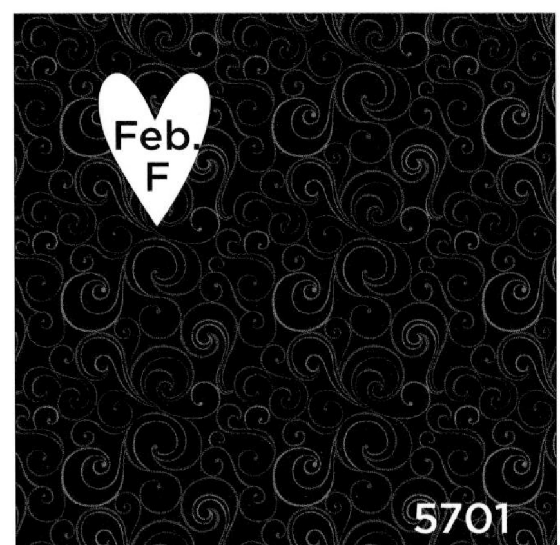

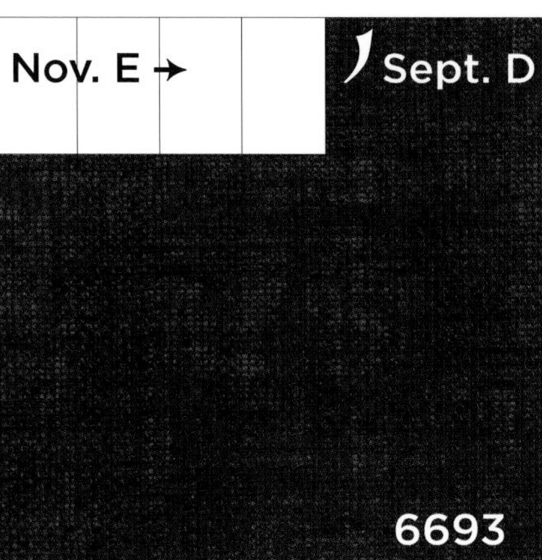

Binding (for all Itty Bitty Quilts)

May J

June E

Oct. E

¾ yard of 3908 Solid – Black
Not included in the Itty Bitty Stack

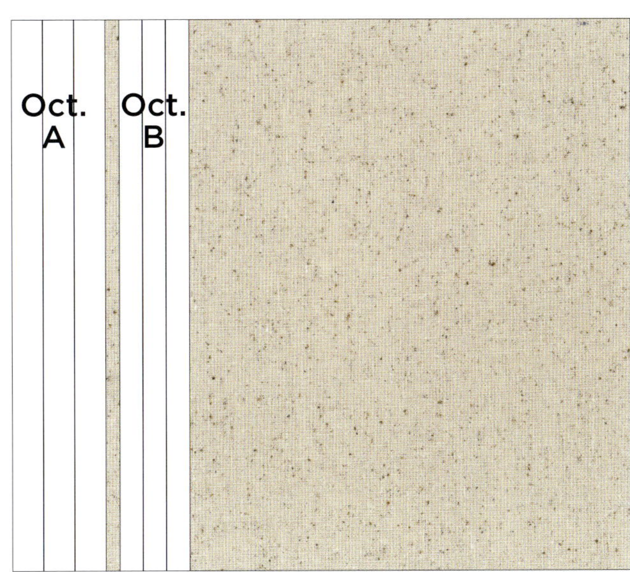

FQ of 7690 Osnaburg – Natural
Not included in the Itty Bitty Stack

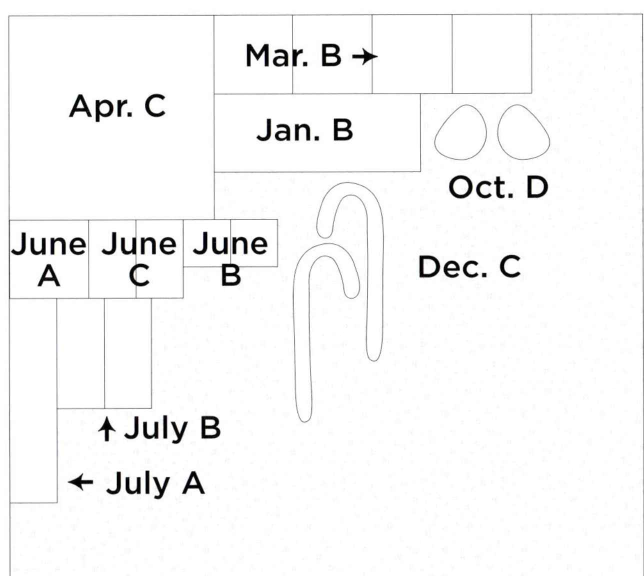

FQ of 6685 Lotta Dots - White on White
Not included in the Itty Bitty Stack

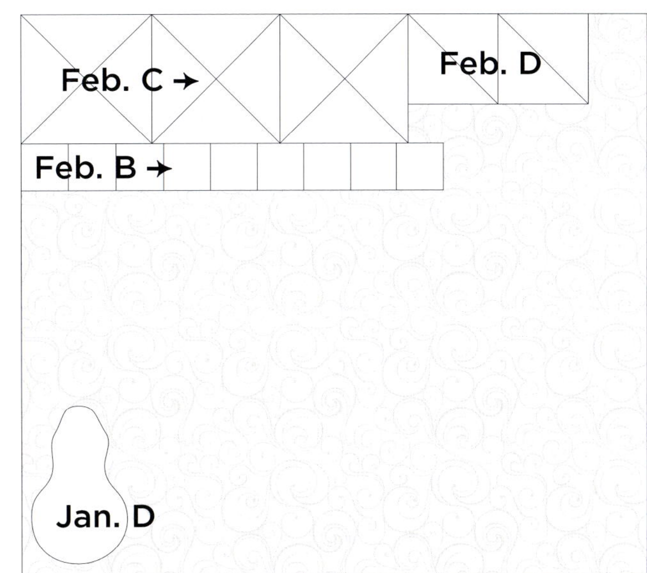

FQ of 5714 Swirls - White on White
Not included in the Itty Bitty Stack

Templates

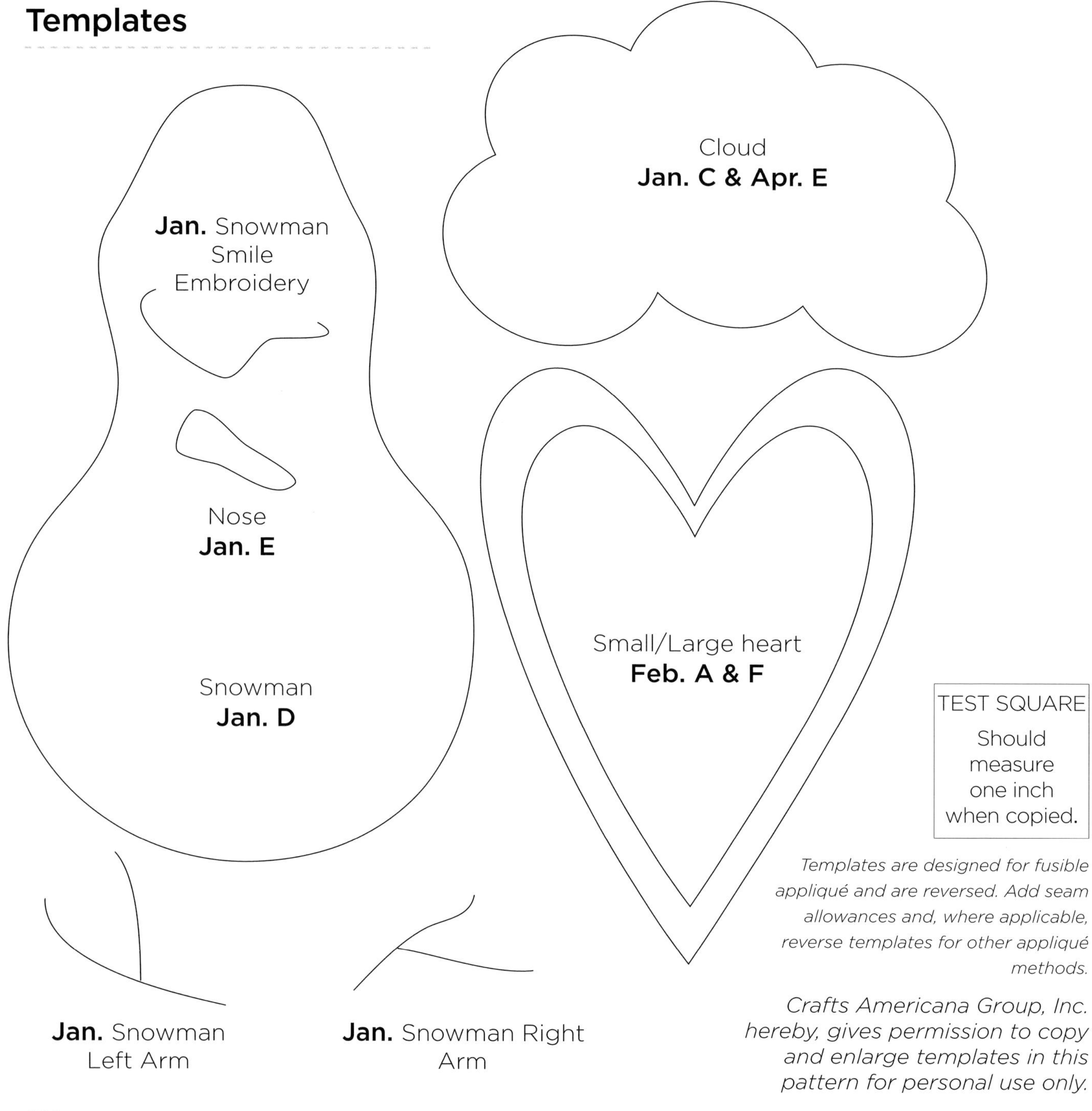

TEST SQUARE

Should measure one inch when copied.

Templates are designed for fusible appliqué and are reversed. Add seam allowances and, where applicable, reverse templates for other appliqué methods.

Templates

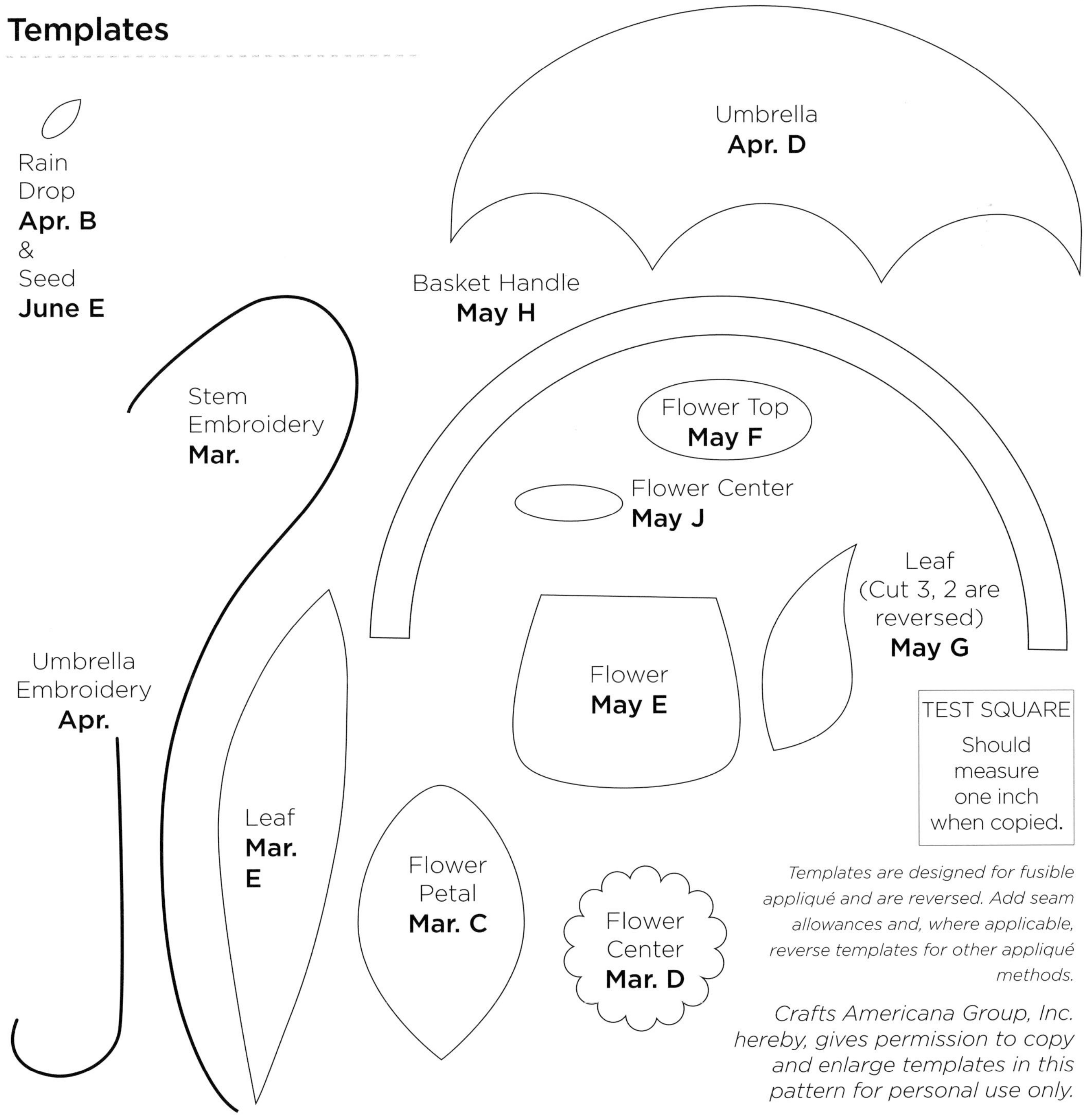

Templates are designed for fusible appliqué and are reversed. Add seam allowances and, where applicable, reverse templates for other appliqué methods.

Templates

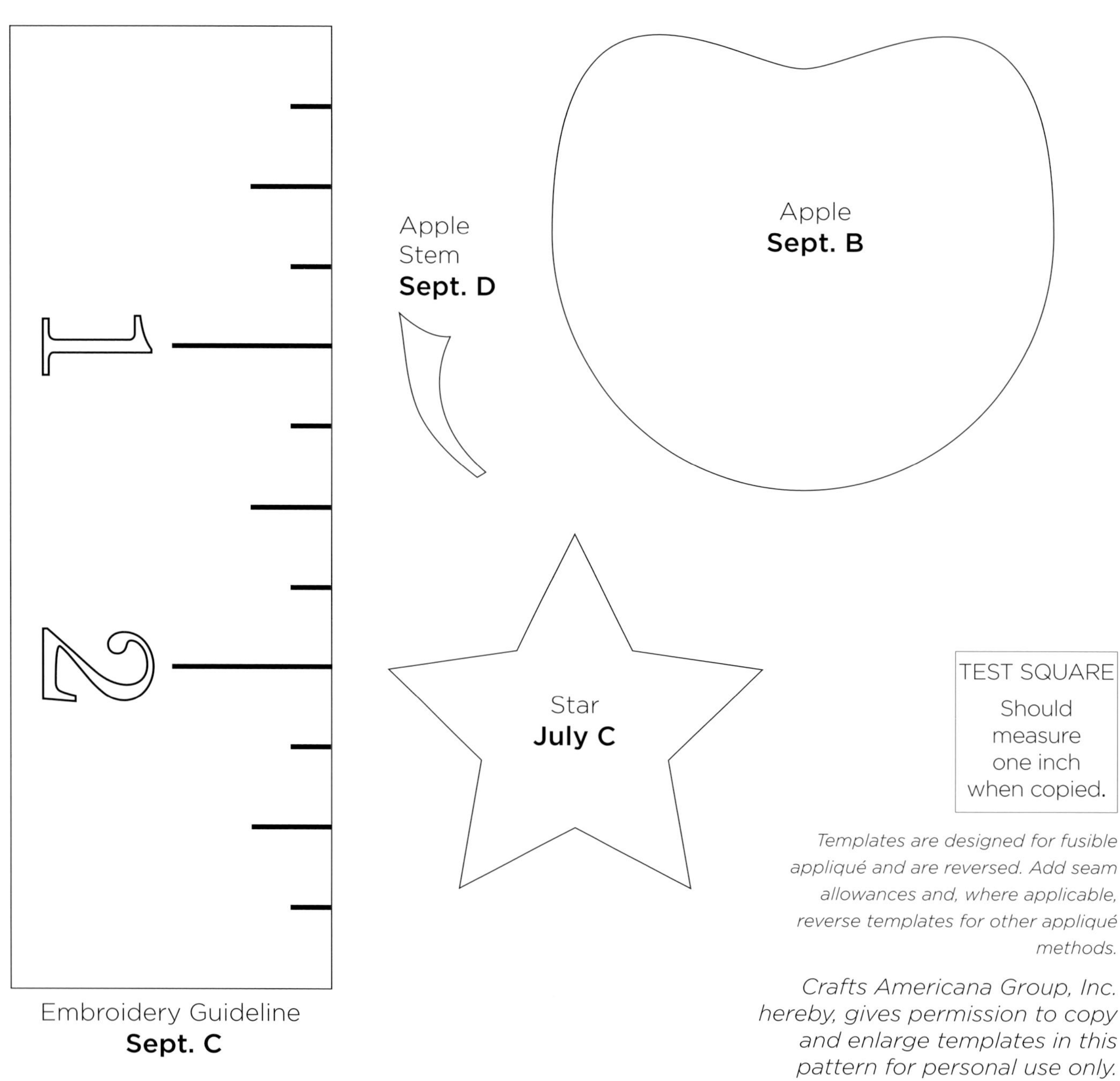

Templates are designed for fusible appliqué and are reversed. Add seam allowances and, where applicable, reverse templates for other appliqué methods.

Templates

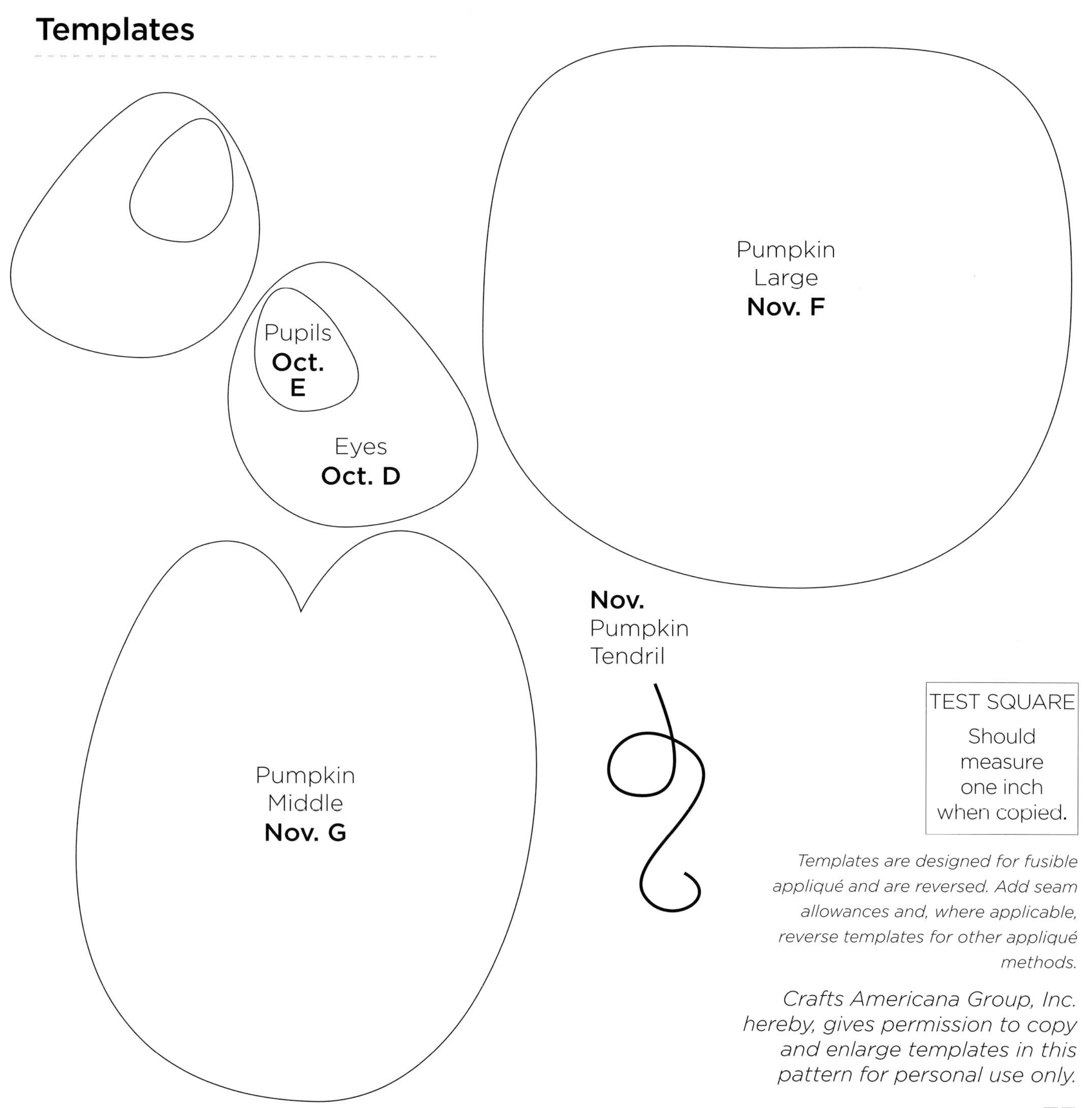

Templates are designed for fusible appliqué and are reversed. Add seam allowances and, where applicable, reverse templates for other appliqué methods.

Templates

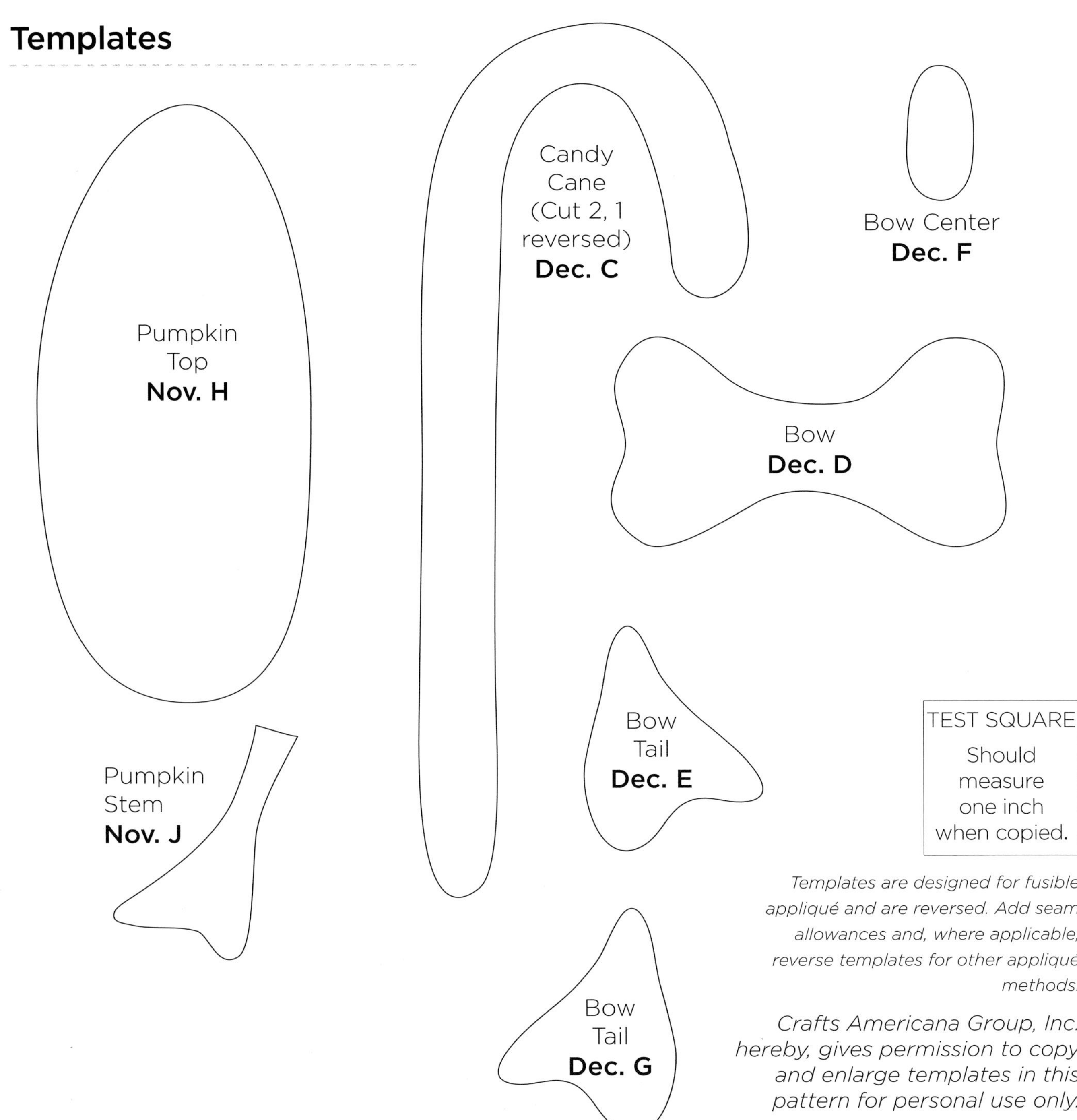

Templates are designed for fusible appliqué and are reversed. Add seam allowances and, where applicable, reverse templates for other appliqué methods.

Bonus!

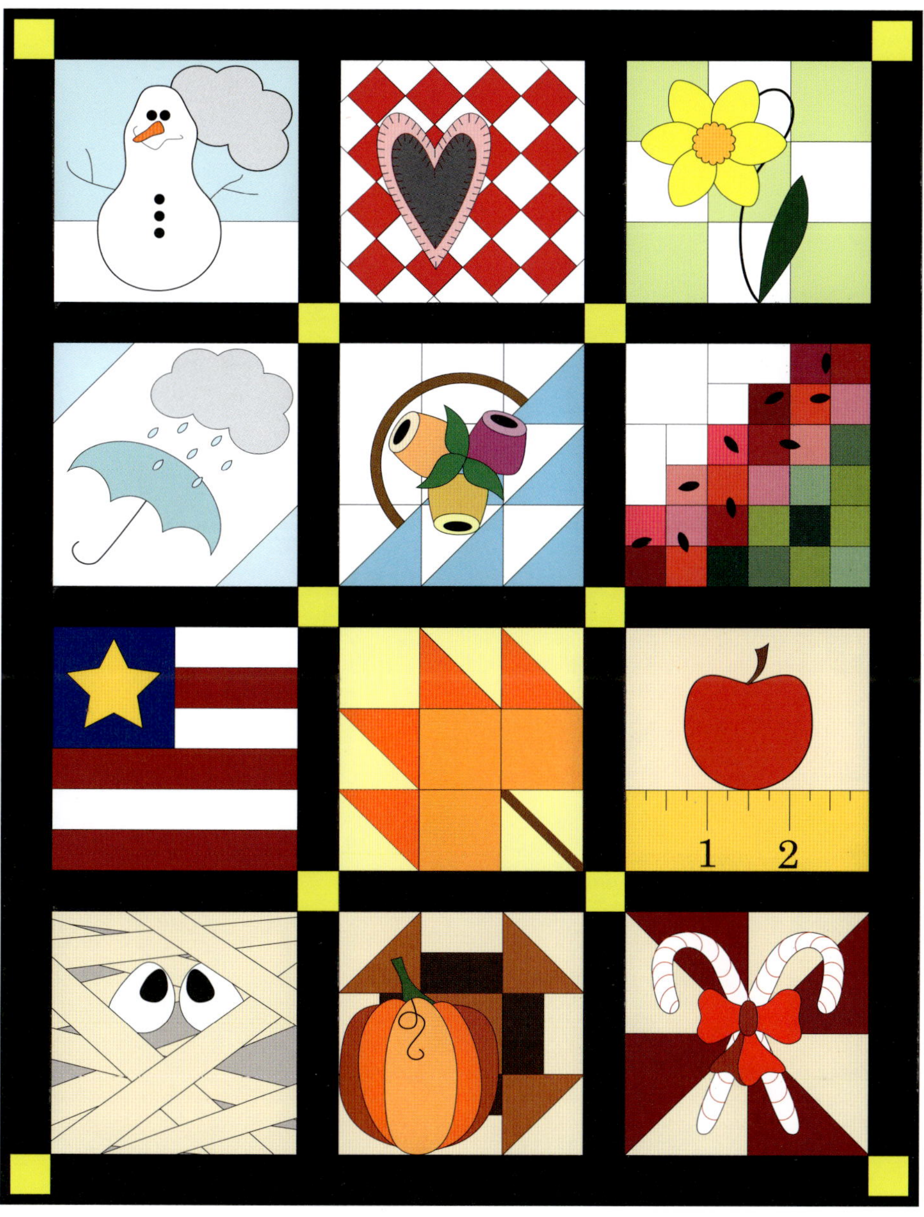

Turn all of your Itty Bitty Quilts into a cheery wall hanging or quilt! Just add your own sashing and corner stones, or come up with your own idea and share it with us! Post your progress on Facebook or Instagram and use hashtag #ittybittyquilts.

We love this stand for displaying Itty Bitty Quilts in style!

Wire Scalloped Single Stand - Grey

Display your mini quilts or individual quilt blocks with this table top display rack. Let your work speak loud and clear with the attractive scalloped design. Hang pieces up to 6½" wide. Grey color. Measures 7½" x 9½"

71445 Retail $19.80 **Your Cost $15.84** *Save 20%*

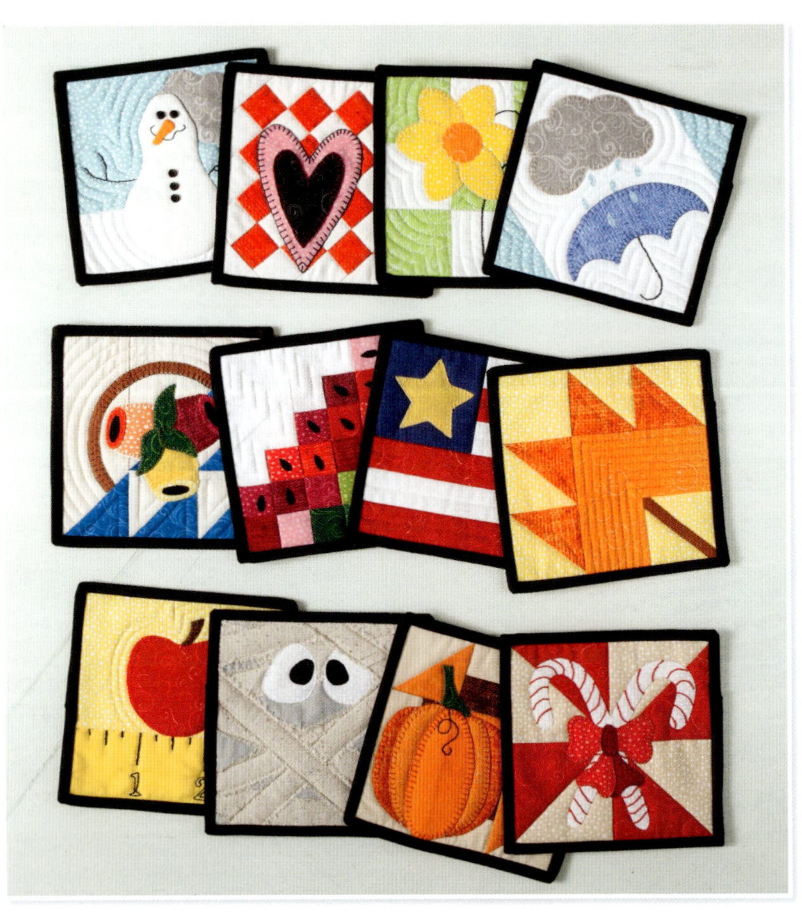

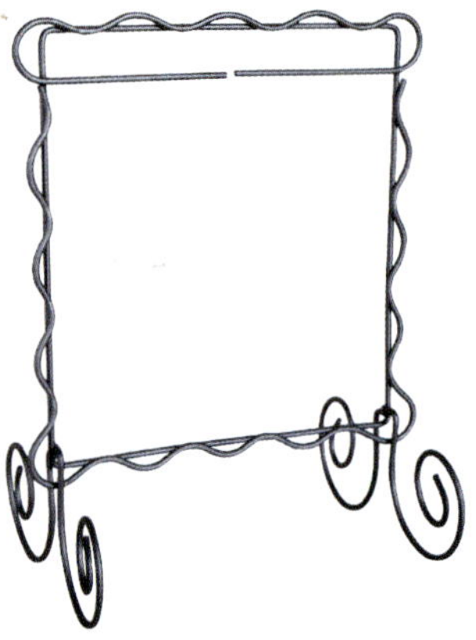